My Journey with Twin Angels

An inspirational story of hope for mothers with special needs
children and their loved ones.

Gifty Kwaku-Addison

AUTHENTIC
WORTH

MY JOURNEY WITH TWIN ANGELS
An inspirational story of hope for mothers with special needs children and their loved ones.

Paperback ISBN: 978-1-7396607-4-1
E-book ISBN: 978-1-7396607-5-8

Published with Authentic Worth
Website: www.authenticworth.com
Email: info@authenticworth.com

Authentic Worth is bringing worth back into you through storytelling and book writing!

Dedication

I give thanks to my Heavenly Father for His strength and wisdom in helping me to write and publish my book.

I dedicate this book in loving memory of my parents; Mr Felix Adjei-Addison and Christine Adjei-Addison (nee Barnes).

My Brother; Michael Abeku Adjei-Addison. Wherever you are in this world, I've written this for you.

To all parents worldwide who are challenged, miserable, mentally and physically drained, overwhelmed and isolated when raising children with disabilities; be encouraged and know that you are not alone on this journey.

Much love to my babies, my world and my 'Dynamic Duo'. You are both beautiful inside and out in unique ways. Despite the tears, challenges, meltdowns and out-of-window routines, I am incredibly grateful and blessed to be your mother. You both continue to inspire me daily. The warmth of your smiles are simply contagious, and I am glad to be holding your hands through this incredible journey. I love you unconditionally because you are both unique and my Crown of Jewels.

To my beautiful family; Chris, Kirsten and Khaela; my number one fans. I could not walk this journey alone. Thank you for never letting me give up and continuing to be my source of hope and inspiration.

To Esther Jacob and the Authentic Worth Publishing Team; thank you for encouraging and helping me to birth my dream.

To my wonderful and supportive circle of friends who have become family; thank you.

Contents Page

Foreword

Gee's life has been a rollercoaster of a ride. In telling her story, she takes us from the dream of her family to the stark reality; from the depths of despair to hope. By sharing her personal account, she permits us to walk in her shoes for a moment and to see things from her perspective.

Ultimately, her story is one of inspiration. Over time, she has discovered that there may not always be light at the end of the tunnel, especially if you don't know if the tunnel will even have an ending! However, there will always be light *in* the tunnel. The challenge is to take the time to pause and find the light, and then focus on that light as you keep on walking. Instead of looking ahead to block out the present, we can find grace in the moment and delight in the small things, even during times of great tragedy.

Entwined throughout the telling of her personal story, Gee gives clarity on the kind of support friends and family can give. Listening to some of the words spoken to her by well-meaning friends whilst she was in the depth of despair is almost farcical. Seeing the simple acts of kindness and concern from others that made the journey bearable provided a road map for the kind of support we ought to give people in our community, whatever burden they are carrying.

If you are on the journey of handling children with additional needs or you know someone who is, this book will give invaluable insights, but above all, hope. Not the glossy hope that ignores reality, but the gritty hope that overcomes and reveals something beautiful in the midst of pain and tragedy.

I am so thankful to know Gee, Chris and their four beautiful girls and to have seen them find hope in the most challenging of circumstances. Their journey has made their family stronger and this is a credit to each one of them who have all had to dig deep to find strength and learn to hold on to God throughout the journey.

1

My Journey with Twin Angels

It has also strengthened me as I have watched them cling to the Lord over the years. It is for this reason that I am constantly inspired by them and honoured to count this family among our closest friends.

Olly Goldenberg
Children Can
November 2022

Preface

Every child is gifted; they just unwrap their packages at different times.

Unknown.

Welcome to an extraordinary journey of a lifetime...

On this unplanned rollercoaster ride, the primary goal for us as parents is to ensure that our children are happy, healthy and allowed to thrive and excel on their terms. As for us, we will cherish the significant milestones and incredible memories in our hearts forever. In some rural areas within Africa, many children who are born with deformities are labelled as 'spirit children, abandoned or killed at birth.' Unfortunately, there are no records of such killings and are often shrouded in secrecy.

The logic behind not keeping deformed children is simple; there aren't friendly environments to support their upbringing, so the best way to deal with such conditions is to take the child's life at birth. Most parents who have children with disabilities often don't see the essence of educating these children, and instead, hide them away from the world, ashamed of the stigma society has created concerning children with disabilities.

The stigma associated with having children in any form of disability affects some of us who have left Africa to live in the Western countries. We are often in denial and tend to attribute every situation to negativity, often refusing to get help for our children.

No expectant mother plans to have a sick child. As soon as one becomes aware that they are pregnant, the excitement sets in, and one starts to plan and build hopes, dreams and expectations for the unborn child. Unfortunately, when the new born arrives, parents won't ever forget their initial diagnosis of an illness or disability as it wasn't meant to be part of the plan.

My Journey with Twin Angels

Although compassionate and well-meaning health professionals, teachers, health visitors and therapists try to provide emotional support and valuable information, most parents describe a feeling of grief and isolation with emotions they find difficult to put into words.

Many parents and professionals have suggested that diagnosing a child's disability initiates a mourning process, much like the grief felt when a child passes away. Yet, in our case, the children are alive, so we must find the strength to care for them and ensure that they thrive, despite the odds stacked against them.

I started writing my story in 2009, and during that time, my trauma was so significant I couldn't get past writing a few sentences before breaking down. I had to tell my story, and as the years went by, I prayed for strength, knowledge and wisdom for God to use me as a voice to reach others going through complicated circumstances, just as I am. I've written this book as a form of therapy, a way to cope with my pain, challenges and immense frustrations of raising daughters with Autism and Epilepsy in a society focused on normalcy.

I am sharing my story to hopefully encourage you to have a renewed mindset and attitude in dealing with daily challenges. This book serves as a reminder that every form of disability can also bring fulfilment and joy.

My story is about trauma, beauty, tears, hopelessness, and hope. I write amid my brokenness and darkest moments, yet; I can say at the same time, there has been significant growth, and I have kept a hopeful heart throughout my journey.

If you decide to read this book despite not caring for a loved one with additional needs, I hope that not only will my story make you feel immense gratitude for not having to deal with any of these issues, but will challenge, inspire and encourage you in all aspects of life to redefine your purpose, dare to be different and dare to dream.

I AM THE CHILD

I am the child who cannot talk
You often pity me; I see it in your eyes
You wonder how much I am aware of — I see that as well
I am aware of much; whether you are happy, sad or fearful,
patient or impatient, full of love and desire,
or if you are just doing your duty by me.

I marvel at your frustration, knowing mine to be far greater,
for I cannot express myself or my needs as you do
You cannot conceive my isolation, so complete, it is at times
I do not gift you with clever conversation, cute remarks to be
laughed over and repeated
I do not give you answers to your everyday questions,
responses over my wellbeing, sharing my needs,
or comments to the world about me.

I do not give you rewards defined by the world's standards — great
strides in development that you can credit yourself
I do not give you understanding as you know it
What I give you is so much more valuable — I give you
opportunities
Opportunities to discover the depth of your character, not mine;
the depth of your love, your commitment, your patience, your
abilities; the opportunity to explore your spirit more deeply than
you imagined possible
I drive you further than you would ever go on your own; working
harder, seeking answers to your many questions with no answers.

I am the child who cannot talk.
I am the child who cannot walk
The world seems to pass me by
You see the longing in my eyes to get out of this chair,
to run and play like the other children
There is so much you take for granted
I want the toys on the shelf, I need to go to the bathroom;
Oh, I've dropped my fork again!

5

My Journey with Twin Angels

I am dependent on you in these ways.
My gift to you is to make you more aware of your great fortune,
your healthy back and legs, your ability to do for yourself
Sometimes, people appear not to notice me; however, I always notice them
I feel not so much envy as desire; the desire to stand upright,
to put one foot in front of the other; to be *independent*
I give you awareness.

I am the child who cannot walk
I am the child who is mentally impaired
I don't learn easily; if you judge me by the world's measuring stick,
what I do know is infinite joy in simple things
I am not burdened as you are with the strife's and conflicts of a more complicated life.
My gift to you is to grant you freedom to enjoy things as a child,
to teach you how much your arms around me mean; to give you love
I give you the gift of simplicity.

I am the child who is mentally impaired
I am the disabled child
I am your teacher. If you allow me,
I will teach you what is really important in life
I will give and teach you unconditional love
I gift you with my innocent trust; my dependency upon you.

I teach you about how precious this life is and about not taking things for granted.
I teach you about forgetting your own needs, desires and dreams.
I teach you giving.
Most of all, I teach you hope and faith.
I am the disabled child.

Author Unknown.

Chapter ONE

-

The Beginning

Being a mother is learning about the strengths you didn't know you had and dealing with fears you didn't know existed.

Linda Wooten.

In April 2007, the death of my mother was one of the hardest things I've ever had to endure. Shortly afterwards, we lost my father-in-law. I laid on my bed one night, staring into the darkness trying to figure out what was good about my life. It had been one disaster after another, and I was sick and tired of it all. I threw myself into the emotional preparations to travel back to Ghana for his funeral to keep myself busy. I was exhausted from the relentless sorrow plaguing me since I lost my beloved mum.

On the day of his burial, I lifted my eyes to the heavens and cried my heart out saying to God; "Surely, we deserve some happiness; some light. We can't be living in darkness all the time. This sorrow is just too much!" My father-in-law was given a befitting military send-off, and soon, we were on our way back to the UK to continue with our lives. After a few months of dealing with unending painful events, I discovered I was pregnant.

First of all, everything seemed different with this pregnancy. There was more fatigue and my tummy was huge. During our first ultrasound at 20 weeks, we could hardly wait to arrive at the hospital. When Chris and I were called into the small room with the sonographer, there was silence as the lady placed the handheld probe on my skin and moved it over my belly.

The black and white images immediately emerged on the small tv screen in front of us. We watched, mesmerised as we realised that there was not only one head, but two.

7

My Journey with Twin Angels

After a series of hums and smiles, the sonographer confirmed that we were not only having one baby, but two. Imagine how elated I was and thought, 'Wow! Some good news at last!' No sooner had that thought crossed my mind; then the room went silent. I suffered a slight panic attack on the examining bed, immediately overwhelmed with the additional concerns that could come with twin pregnancies. From where I lay on the examining bed, I could tell that Chris was in shock, but I had no idea what was going through his mind.

I staggered my way off the bed and the fears started emerging in the form of tears. I was terrified, and my mind was racing at about 1,000 miles per hour. I thought of our turquoise Peugeot 206 sitting on the driveway which hardly had enough room to carry myself, Chris and the two big girls. Visions of us all cramped in our tiny 2-bed flat flashed through my mind and I panicked at the sheer thought of having two additions to the family.

By this point, tears started rolling down my cheeks. After a few minutes of silence, Chris gave me a knowing smile. We talked and he reassured me that things would be just fine and the excitement overrode the doubt and fear. It almost felt too good to be true! We felt blessed and went back home with pure joy and started preparing for the arrival of our two precious angels. We had budgets and plans to make in buying two of everything. Exciting times, or so, we thought.

The first couple of months of my pregnancy were a dream. I couldn't exercise as much as I would've loved to, so I walked when I could, took good care of myself and ate healthy meals. Nonetheless, there were nights where I would wake up craving omelettes or foods which took ages to make or we would have to drive all the way to North London, however, I managed to keep those in check. Apart from the occasional nausea and fatigue, I had no major issues or concerns, not even a day of morning sickness.

I didn't know what my precious babies would look like or what they'd grow up to be, but I knew that I loved them with every fibre of my being. I was convinced that just like my other girls, they would be world-changers and were destined for greatness. I couldn't wait to meet them. At each monthly check-up, the doctor and nurses were always expressing their happiness with my progress. Then; one day, everything changed. During one of my routine appointments, the doctor in his long white coat had a look of seriousness about him after running a series of tests.

He knew that something wasn't quite right and asked for more ultrasound scans to be conducted. I will never forget how I felt and the yellow walls of the room that day. Several scans later, it was detected that my special babies whom I'd developed an enormous bond with were not growing. It was as though the world had stopped for me and time stood still. I was in a state of shock! My perfect miracle twin pregnancy hadn't gone as I'd hoped. The doctor instructed that I had to come to the hospital every other day so my girls could be monitored.

Our lives came crashing down around us at what was supposed to be the happiest time of our lives. In that very instant, our lives were changed forever. There were tears; lots of them. This could not be. What happened to my prayers and childhood dream of having perfect babies?

After a few weeks of monitoring, the situation remained unchanged. There were still no improvements to their growth and I was on steroid injections to strengthen their lungs in case they were to be delivered early. I had needle phobias since I was a little girl, so the sight of needles was enough for me to break out in a sweat.

I was extremely anxious; however, we were assured that the steroids would speed up the development of the girls' lungs and give them a much better chance of survival. At 34 weeks into the pregnancy, consultants decided that my two angels had to be delivered by a caesarean section (C-section) as the situation with their weight was not improving.

On the morning of Tuesday 26th August 2008, I woke up filled with joy knowing I was going to meet my angels, but also filled with dread as I didn't know the challenges of their failure to thrive, as doctors described them, would cost the family. The C-section went smoothly as planned and Ivana was born weighing 1.4kg closely followed by her twin sister; Jane weighing 1.6kg. My amazing angels were born at 34 weeks at the Royal Free Hospital in London. Chris, who had been keeping an eagle eye on the doctors noticed that Ivana had stopped breathing. Immediately, it felt as though all the air had been sucked from the room and I could sense the panic and growing tension.

The energy was tense and I was unsure of exactly what was happening around me. Everything happened so fast that I'd expected to be cradling my new-born babies; instead, I lay in the recovery room, overwhelmed by fear and disbelief. Suddenly, from where I lay on the operating table, alarms sounded in my ears and I saw a frenzy of doctors and nurses rushing about trying to save my precious baby. I lay there helplessly watching, praying and willing for my baby to live. Our *birth plan* didn't include this and the pain was so unbearable. It was much more than I could endure.

Eventually, the doctors were able to resuscitate Ivana. I'd been told they'd stopped growing in my womb at 20 weeks, but nothing could have prepared me as a mother or my family for the subsequent trials and great difficulties we would encounter. I had a dream to have perfectly normal twin angels, but that didn't happen.

There were no balloons or flowers and my hopes and dreams of friends and family welcoming our girls into the world were crushed. As a child, I'd always dreamt of having beautiful, healthy children, and in that instant, the dream was taken away from me. The pain will never go away because in that moment, the loss of my childhood dream was very significant.

Chapter TWO

-

Grieving the Loss of a Childhood Dream

With tremendous burdens often come enormous gifts. The trick is to identify the gifts and glory in them.

Dr. Maya Shetreat-Klein.

What should've been a beautiful day filled with joy and laughter for our family quickly became an evolving nightmare. We were wheeled into the labour ward later that evening, and in true typical hospital style, the nurses announced that family members couldn't stay past 7.00pm, so sadly, Chris and the children had to leave the hospital.

Later that night, Ivana started to make a grunting sound. I pressed the buzzer to alert the nurses on duty but was told there were staff shortages so I had to be patient. Finally, as the grunting sounds got louder, I caused enough commotion for the nurses on duty to take note and immediately rush my baby to the neonatal unit. Minutes later, Jane started making the same grunting noise and was also rushed to the neonatal unit; then, the nightmare began.

Chris arrived at the hospital the following morning with a spring in his step, waiting to see his beloved new-born baby girls. He was, however, re-directed to the neonatal unit where his precious girls had spent the night. The days and weeks that followed were one of the most agonising we've ever endured. With tubes coming out of their noses and almost every part of their body one can think of, our tiny babies were in incubators fighting for their lives as we stood by and watched helplessly.

I'd lost a lot of blood during delivery, but all of that became secondary as I struggled to come to terms with what was unfolding before our eyes. Loved ones prayed fervently for our babies as they

11

lay in the neonatal unit fighting for their lives. Olly, the officiating pastor at our wedding who'd become a very good friend of the family, was the first to come to the hospital and sit, pray, support and encourage us. Then, another good friend came to the hospital and the grief and pain she was experiencing was almost too much to bear. Inevitably, she broke down. I saw her shaking with fear and that scene would stay with me forever. It was particularly difficult for me because I had another friend who had a baby boy on the same day.

While I was happy that her delivery went smoothly and she'd delivered a healthy baby, I was in deep shock, broken, and had many questions. For me, that was when reality of the whole situation hit. *'God; what is happening to my babies?'* I screamed silently within myself. I held them and wept as I sang Don Moen's song *"I am the God that healeth thee."* They were tiny, didn't have much hair as I'd hoped, but they had the most beautiful, slender fingers and toes. They were beautiful, and I prayed that God would save them and wake me up from this nightmare of a dream.

Parking at the hospital was costly, so we agreed on a routine whereby I'd stay with my girls during the day, and Chris would stay with them at night in the neonatal unit. He would sit there praying for not only our girls, but also the other babies in the neonatal unit fighting for their lives. One night, as he sat patiently by our girls, a nurse entered and with an icy tone, asked him; "What are you doing here? There's nothing you can do for your girls; just go home to bed!" Her tone shocked him. Was it not part of their job to be comforting and kind?

I loved to breastfeed my children and vowed that I was going to breastfeed them no matter what. It was one of those days where I sat quietly in a waiting room, expressing my milk and trying to digest all the happenings of the last few days that another nurse came in and, without sympathy, advised me to stop wasting my time because my girls would never be able to have my milk and will live on special milk and dietary requirements for the rest of their lives.

My Journey with Twin Angels

The next day, as the doctor came on his rounds, he said to us; "Of all the children I've known to have this condition, none have lived past the age of 1!" Additional needs, handicapped, disabled, failure to thrive, global developmental delay, sickness, chronically illness, and metabolic acidosis were some of the predictions for my angels. What a dreadful day that was!

I started conducting research into these conditions. However, once I came across the word *rigor mortis*; a term which signified death, I stopped searching as I couldn't bear the doom and gloom the research articles were bringing up. The doctors and nurses added to our anguish as they began to pronounce negativity about the future of our girls.

According to the doctors at the Royal Free Hospital, they didn't have the medical expertise to treat the girls, and there were a series of meetings and consultations with various doctors at Great Ormond Street to try and find beds for the girls. Unfortunately, Great Ormond Street was unable to accommodate them, so a decision was made to take them to another hospital. At the same time, doctors collaborated with top experts and consultants to save our girls.

I do not recall whether I was fully discharged from the hospital; all I could think about were my beautiful baby girls fighting for their lives. The girls were still in incubators in the neonatal unit at this point, and we were told that as their bodies had high levels of *lactate*; a condition known as Lactic Acidosis, we were unable to feed them and would have to wait until doctors could determine what was going on in their little bodies.

I was, however, determined to breastfeed and persisted in expressing my breast milk daily for Chris to take home and freeze for our angels. I knew that we could freeze them for months, and hoped that one day, despite the naysayers, I would feed the girl's milk. Lactic acidosis in layman's terms is when acid builds up in the bloodstream faster than it can be removed. Lactic acid is produced when oxygen levels in the body drop. The most common cause of lactic acidosis is *intense exercise*. However, it can also be caused by certain diseases such as AIDS, cancer, kidney failure, respiratory failure and sepsis.

Symptoms may include:
- Nausea
- Weakness
- A blood test to check electrolyte levels

The condition typically occurs when cells receive too little oxygen (hypoxia), for example, during vigorous exercise. In this situation, impaired cellular respiration leads to lower pH levels. Simultaneously, cells are forced to metabolise glucose anaerobically, which leads to lactate formation. Therefore, elevated lactate indicates tissue hypoxia, hypo perfusion, and possible damage.

Lactic acidosis is a consequence of the processes causing Rigor Mortis. In Latin terms:

1) **Rigor** also known as *stiffness*
2) **Mortis** also known as *death*

is one of the recognisable signs of decease caused by chemical changes in the muscles, causing the limbs of the corpse to stiffen.[1]

In the absence of oxygen, tissue in the muscles of the deceased carry out anaerobic metabolism using muscle glycogen as the energy source causing acidification. With the depletion of muscle glycogen, the loss of ATP causes the muscles to grow stiff, as the actin-myosin bonds cannot be released. Rigor is later resolved by enzymatic breakdown of the myofibers. They were eventually diagnosed as having *Metabolic Acidosis*. Metabolic acidosis is a condition which there is too much acid in the body fluids.

Causes
Metabolic acidosis occurs when the body produces too much acid, or when the kidneys aren't removing enough acid from the body. There are several types of metabolic acidosis:

- **Diabetic acidosis** (also called diabetic ketoacidosis and DKA): Develops when acidic substances known as ketone builds up in the body. This occurs with uncontrolled type 1 diabetes.

- **Hyperchloremic acidosis**: Results from excessive loss of sodium bicarbonate from the body and can occur with severe diarrhoea.

Lactic Acidosis results from a build-up of lactic acid. It can be caused by the following:
- Alcohol
- Cancer
- Exercising intensely
- Liver failure
- Medications, such as salicylates
- Prolonged lack of oxygen from shock, heart failure, or severe anaemia
- Seizures

Other causes of metabolic acidosis include:
- Kidney disease (distal renal tubular acidosis and proximal renal tubular acidosis)
- Poisoning by aspirin, ethylene glycol (found in antifreeze), or methanol
- Severe dehydration

Symptoms
Most symptoms are caused by the underlying disease or condition that causes the metabolic acidosis. Metabolic acidosis itself usually causes rapid breathing. Confusion or lethargy may also occur. Severe metabolic acidosis can lead to shock or death. In some situations, metabolic acidosis can be a mild, chronic ongoing condition.

Examinations and Tests
- Arterial blood gas
- Serum electrolytes

- Urine pH

Arterial blood gas analysis and a serum electrolytes test (such as a basic metabolic panel) will confirm acidosis is present and determine whether it is respiratory acidosis or metabolic acidosis. Other tests may be needed to determine the cause of the acidosis.

Treatment
Treatment is aimed at the underlying condition. In some cases, sodium bicarbonate *(the chemical in baking soda)* may be given to reduce the acidity of the blood.

Outlook (Prognosis)
The outlook will depend on the underlying disease causing the condition.

Possible Complications
We were told that the main treatment for acidosis is to correct the underlying medical problem that caused the condition. Finally, we were informed that very severe metabolic acidosis can lead to shock or death.

We live in a society where everything is about perfection; the last thing one wants to do is stand out from the crowd and be different. "How can I carry on as normal?" I asked. We as a family didn't stand a chance; normal was a distant dream.

Parenting special needs children comes with many emotions that can be highly stressful. One of the most difficult for many is the feeling of being in isolation. We tend to pour ourselves into our children's diagnoses and our caregiving roles. We research and talk to experts, doctors, school counsellors, therapists, and special education professionals; all to ensure that our children have the best life possible.

Chapter THREE

-

The Existence of Angels

Angels are all around us, all the time, in the very air we breathe.

Eileen Elias Freeman.

After the 9th day of being in the hospital waiting for a transfer to Great Ormond Street, we were told there were still no beds available. Instead, Ivana and Jane were transferred by an air ambulance to the University College Hospital in Euston. The special care baby unit seemed very strange.

As soon as you entered, the air was stale, the ward was very hostile, and the nurses on duty avoided all eye contact. As I observed these nurses, I immediately wondered why they avoided eye contact. I thought they were doing that because they feared the worst and didn't want to be the first to break the bad news to us.

My little angels were placed in incubators with tubes wired up to them everywhere as they fought for their lives. I was broken to the core, partly because I couldn't clean my babies of all the signs of afterbirth. The vernix had dried up on their skin, but the nurses would not let us near them for a clean as we were told they would be cold which could prove fatal.

Surprisingly, the girls were very active in their incubators and would make all sorts of gymnastic moves, much to the amusement of some of the other parents. They would come to us describing what they saw when we weren't around, making me sick to the pit of my stomach.

As much as I would exchange pleasantries with them and laugh at their jokes, I was silently dying inside. My girls were not having a show in a circus; they were fighting for their lives. One of the friendlier nurses allowed me to attempt to wipe the vernix off their skin with olive oil and water. I honestly cannot say how we made it through as a family during those bleak days. Chris, on the other hand, used this time as an opportunity to encourage and pray with the parents at the hospital for the same reasons and to top that, some special friendships were made around that time.

One day, as I wandered around at the hospital in a world of my own, I stumbled across a lady sitting sadly in a corner. I approached her and we started chatting away. She had such a calm demeanour that was effortless for us to sit and share our frustrations. She had also given birth to twins; however, one had fluid in her head and would require an operation. That was the beginning of our friendship. We sat and encouraged each other for a while then went our separate ways. We've remained friends to this day.

Around that time, we also learnt about a method called *"Kangaroo Care."* Studies state that in the early 1980s, the mortality rate for premature infants in Bogota, Colombia was 70%. The babies were dying of infections and respiratory problems, as well as lack of attention paid to them by a bonded parent. Kangaroo care for these infants evolved out of necessity. Mothers of premature infants were given their babies to hold 24 hours a day. They slept with them and tucked them under their clothing as if in a kangaroo's pouch. If a baby needed oxygen, it was administered under an oxygen hood placed on the mother's chest.

Doctors who conducted a concurrent study of the kangaroo care noticed a precipitous drop in neonatal mortality. Babies were not only surviving, but they were also thriving. In Bogota, babies who were born as early as 10 weeks before their due date were going home within 24 hours. The criterion for these babies is that they will live and breathe on their own and able to suck. However, their weight is followed closely and they can be gavage-fed if necessary.

Dr. Susan Ludington is one of the people that's been most instrumental in bringing kangaroo care to the United States and around the world. She's been intimately involved in many research projects, and her work is having a powerful, positive impact on premature babies and their families.

According to research, the few hospitals that regularly use kangaroo care protocols have mothers or fathers carry their babies for 2 to 3 hours per day, skin-to-skin. The baby is naked except for a diaper and something must cover his or her back; either the parent's clothing or receiving a blanket folded in quarters. The baby is mostly in an upright position against the parent's chest.

The benefits of kangaroo care are numerous including the following:

- The baby having a stable heart rate (no bradycardia)
- More regular breathing (a 75% decrease in apnoeic episodes)
- Improved oxygen saturation levels
- No cold stress
- Longer periods of sleep
- More rapid weight gain
- More rapid brain development
- Reduction of purposeless activity
- Decreased crying
- Longer periods of alertness
- More successful breastfeeding episodes
- Earlier hospital discharge

The benefits to the parents include closure over having a baby in NICU; feeling close to their babies (earlier bonding); having confidence that they can care for their baby even better than hospital staff; gaining confidence that their baby is well cared for and feeling in control, not to mention significantly; decreased cost!

According to research, one of the first things to happen is that maintenance of the baby's body temperature begins to depend on the mother, requiring the baby to use fewer calories to stay warm. Mothers naturally modulate the warmth of their breasts to keep their infants at the optimal temperature where babies sleep best, have good oxygen saturation levels, the least caloric expenditure, and so forth. Maternal breast temperature can rise rapidly, then fall off as the baby is warm. As the baby starts to cool, the breasts heat up again as much as 2 degrees Celsius in two minutes.

Being next to the mother also helps the baby regulate his or her respiratory heart rates. Babies experience significantly less bradycardia and often, none at all, and the respiratory rate of kangarooed infants becomes more stable. The depth of each breath becomes more and apnoea decreases fourfold and often disappears altogether. If apnoeic episodes occur, the length of each episode decreases. During kangaroo care, a premature baby's overall growth rate increases. This is in part due to the baby's ability to sleep, thus conserving energy and putting caloric expenditure towards growth.

According to Dr. Ludington, during the last 6 weeks of pregnancy, babies sleep 20 to 22 hours per day. In a typical NICU, however, they spend less than two hours total in deep, quiet sleep. Most of that comes in 10 or 20 second snatches. With kangaroo care, the infant typically snuggles into the breasts and are deep in sleep within just a few minutes. These babies gain weight faster than their non-kangarooed counterparts, and it's interesting to note that they usually don't lose any of their birth weight.

Researchers have gained significant insight into what happens to an infant's brain during kangaroo care. Any baby's heart and respiratory rates can be plotted as an artistic drawing. Because premature infants lack the ability to coordinate their breathing and heart rates, the rates plot out as chaotic. This means that with increased demand on the cardiovascular system, as with crying or fussing, the system doesn't respond with related increase in cardiac output.

In other words, the baby's respiratory rate may increase while crying, but the heart rate doesn't. As preterm babies mature, these rates become synchronised or coupled, resulting in an orderly drawing when the rates are plotted together, the drawing no longer looks random.

According to researchers, infants in kangaroo care found that coupling occurs after only 10 minutes. This hardly seemed possible because it equalled 4 weeks of brain development in the normal preterm baby. However, as researchers studied brain wave patterns of infants in kangaroo care, they found two critical things:

- **First**; there's a doubling of alpha waves; the brain wave pattern associated with contentment and bliss

- **Second**; they found that *delta brushes* were occurring. Delta brushes happen only when new synapses are being formed. So, holding the infant skin-to-skin allows his or her brain to continue developing neural synapses

Imagine the implications if all infants at risk were kangarooed. Dr. Ludington aptly sums up kangaroo care by saying *"Separation not biologically normal."* Knowing enough about kangaroo care to help them make informed decisions is another essential tool for the caregiver's birth bag. All infants benefit from skin-to-skin contact, breastfeeding, and shared sleep; nonetheless, some babies need kangaroo care more severely. They include premature infants with low muscle tone or disabilities, high-need infants, those with intrauterine growth retardation, or those with difficulty gaining weight.

Midwives will do well to learn the basics of kangaroo care and where to turn for further information. Adding Dr. Ludington's book, Kangaroo Care to ones' library is an excellent first step. Being supportive of parents and giving encouragement and positive reinforcement is also very helpful. Remember that sometimes kangaroo care means the difference between life and death.

With this information, Chris and I started *kangarooing* Ivana and Jane. The results were amazing as our babies slowly started to thrive. Then, after days of fervent prayers, one doctor turned to me and asked if I had any stored breastmilk. I was in shock as just the other day, I had been told it was a waste of time to store the milk. However, the doctor said that he was willing to try the reserved milk, and if they threw that up, medical practitioners would have to find other means of getting nutrients into their tiny, fragile bodies.

My Journey with Twin Angels

Chris rushed home to bring some frozen milk, and the nurses started feeding our angels with 1ml of expressed breastmilk at several intervals; however, Ivana and Jane were unable to digest the milk. We were heartbroken and pleaded with the doctors not to give up easily on them as we were confident that God was going to answer our prayers and the milk would be digested.

Each day, I wandered the hallways of the hospital corridor in fear and shock, as well as the overbearing feeling that something very special had been stolen from us. Joy had been stolen. There were little things that should've happened but didn't. The expectations of all the happy visits, flowers and squeals of joy now turned into tears, looks of sadness and expressions of sympathy. We had no other choice but to carry on praying for a breakthrough. God finally answered our prayers in the form of Andrea; the nurse. She was the turning point; she was the mysterious one.

Chris told me on the first day he set eyes on Andrea that she seemed different to all the other nurses and that there was something special about her. Through all my emotions and a barrage of thoughts swirling around in my head, I heard but dismissed the fact that she could truly be special. Andrea, whom we'd never met, was quieter than the other nurses, possibly in her early thirties and had a cheerful manner and a reassuring smile.

That first night when she came on duty, she offered me a tissue to wipe away my tears, took a bowl of water mixed with essential oils and proceeded to wipe my babies with cotton wool to get the hard white crusts that had formed on their bodies. She nursed them with ease and confidence of someone who'd been in the baby business for a long time.

After a while, she turned her attention to me and asked; "How are you feeling about your girls?" I was surprised by the directness of the question but found myself glad for the invitation to pour out my frustrations. Although I am never one to be at a loss for words, I struggled with how to articulate my jumbled thoughts and emotions to a stranger. She gently said; "It's okay to grieve, you know. Parents are allowed to grieve the lost dreams of a perfect child."

22

My Journey with Twin Angels

On that very day, my babies started to digest their food for the first time. Andrea insisted that I go home for some rest as, at this point, I hadn't been home in days. She assured us that she would take good care of the girls while we were away. The girls had been unable to digest any of the milk until this point, and we were apprehensive that they were losing even more weight.

She advised us to go home and take some much-needed rest and call at 7.00pm to check on the girls. Chris called the ward at precisely 7.00pm, and Andrea calmly answered the phone, delivering the good news we'd been praying for. The girls were finally digesting their food; the frozen breastmilk! We were ecstatic and thanked God for answered prayers. Andrea encouraged us that everything would work out for the best.

The next time we saw Andrea was at an MRI scan when I wasn't allowed in the room. Chris had driven off to look for a parking spot, and as I stood helplessly trying to figure out how to carry the two car seats in the hospital, I saw her. Immediately, goose bumps broke out all over my body at the mere sight. She told me that she had a day off, but was inclined to come to the hospital, so she did. She carried Ivana and took each of them in for their scans. I sat waiting helplessly in a corner, watching and willing for my girls to be well even as she put on their clothes with her eyes radiating such love.

Watching this scene tugged at my heartstrings as I felt for a fleeting moment that this woman, whoever she was, deserved these beautiful miracles more than I did as she could take better care of them. Fleetingly, it crossed my mind that she could be an angel. In fact, I can most assuredly say that God sent a guardian angel like Andrea to protect our precious little girls during turbulent times.

We never saw Andrea again. She was there to protect us in our darkest moments. Shortly afterwards, our angels were discharged to Queen Elizabeth Hospital II in Welwyn Garden City, where we were able to give the girls their first proper bath. Uncertain about the future and the life my beautiful babies would have, I threw myself into caring for them. My life had taken a different course and it felt that it was no longer my own.

Chapter FOUR

-

The Diagnosis

A diagnosis can't predict the extraordinary love you have for your child.

Tara McCallan.

I had envisioned a future of my beautiful angels playing with their dolls, attending modern dance classes, wearing identical clothing, applying each other's makeup and building close relationships among themselves and their older siblings. However, that was sadly not meant to be. Due to their severe developmental delay, we constantly clap and celebrate every little milestone in our home.

Unfortunately, we also spent a lot of time in meetings and hospitals and had to undergo assessments for the girls to be in school. After years of early intervention, my precious angels, who were also non-verbal, were diagnosed with a Visual Impairment (certified partially blind) and Global Developmental Delay. Slowly, the signs of Autism began to creep in.

What is Autism Spectrum Disorder (ASD)?
According to the National Autistic Society, Autism is a lifelong developmental disability which affects how people communicate and interact with the world. 1 in 100 people are on the autism spectrum, and there are around 700,000 autistic adults and children in the UK. Autism spectrum disorder (ASD) is a developmental disability caused by differences in the brain.

Some people with ASD have a known difference such as a genetic condition. Other causes are not yet known. Scientists believe there are multiple causes of ASD that act together to change the most common ways people develop. We still have much to learn about these causes and how they impact people with ASD.

People with ASD may behave, communicate, interact, and learn in ways that are different from most other people. There is often nothing about how they look that sets them apart from other people. The abilities of people with ASD can vary significantly. For example, some people with ASD may have advanced conversation skills, whereas others may be nonverbal. Some people with ASD need a lot of help in their daily lives; others can work and live with little to no support.

ASD begins before the age of 3 and can last throughout a person's life, although symptoms may improve over time. Some children show ASD symptoms within the first 12 months of life. In others, symptoms may not show up until 24 months of age or later. Some children with ASD gain new skills and meet developmental milestones around 18-24 months, and then, they stop gaining or lose the skills they once had.

As children with ASD become adolescents and young adults, they may have difficulties developing and maintaining friendships, communicating with peers and adults, or understanding what behaviours are expected in school or on the job. In addition, they may come to the attention of healthcare providers because they also have conditions such as anxiety, depression, or attention-deficit/hyperactivity disorder, which occur more often in people with ASD than in people without ASD.

Autistic people have their own strengths and weaknesses. Below is a list of difficulties they share including two critical challenges required for a diagnosis:

Social Communication and Social Interaction Challenges:

Social Communication
Autistic people have difficulties with interpreting both verbal and non-verbal language such as gestures or tone of voice. Some autistic people are unable to speak or have limited speech while other

autistic people have very good language skills but struggle to understand sarcasm or the tones of voices. Other challenges include:

- Taking things literally and not understanding abstract concepts.
- Needing extra time to process information or answer questions.
- Repeating what others say to them (this is called *echolalia*)

Social Interaction

Autistic people often have difficulty *reading* others – recognising or understanding ones' feelings and intentions to express their own emotions. This can make it very hard to navigate in the social world. Autistic people may:

- Appear to be insensitive
- Seek out time alone when overloaded by others
- Not seek comfort from other people
- Appear to behave *strangely* in a way that's thought to be socially inappropriate
- Finds it hard to form friendships

With its unwritten rules, the world can seem very unpredictable and confusing to autistic people. This is why they often prefer to have routines so they know what's going to happen. For example, they want to travel the same way to and from school or work, wear the same clothes or eat precisely the same food for breakfast.

Autistic people may also repeat movements such as hand flapping, rocking, or the repetitive use of an object such as twirling a pen or opening and closing a door. Autistic people often engage in these behaviours to help calm themselves down when they are stressed or anxious, but many autistic people do it because they find it enjoyable.

Changes to routines can also be very distressing for autistic people and make them very anxious. For example; having to adjust to big events like Christmas or changing schools, facing uncertainty at work, or something simple like a bus diversion that triggers their angst.

Social interaction behaviours may include:

- Making little or inconsistent eye contact
- Appearing not to look at or listen to people who are talking
- Infrequently sharing interest, emotion, or enjoyment of objects and activities (i.e., infrequently pointing or showing things to others)
- Being slow to respond to one's name or other verbal bids for attention
- Having difficulties with back-and-forth conversations
- Talking at length about a favourite subject without noticing that others aren't interested and not giving others a chance to respond
- Displaying facial expressions, movements, and gestures that don't match what is being said
- Having an unusual tone of voice that sounds flat and robot-like
- Having trouble understanding another person's point of view; unable to predict or understand other people's actions
- Difficulties in adjusting to behaviours and social situations
- Difficulties of sharing in imaginative play or making friends

Repetitive and Restrictive Behaviour

With its unwritten rules, the world can seem a very unpredictable and confusing place for autistic people. This is why they often prefer to have routines so they know what's going to happen. Restrictive and repetitive behaviours include the following:

- Having a lasting intense interest in specific topics such as numbers, details, or facts
- Showing overly focused interests such as moving objects
- Becoming upset by slight changes in a routine and having difficulty with transitions
- Being more or less sensitive than other people to sensory input, such as light, sound, clothing, or temperature

People with ASD may also experience sleep problems and irritability. Those with the autism spectrum, on the other hand, may have many strengths, including the following:

- Being able to learn things in detail and remember information for long periods of time
- Being strong visual and auditory learners
- Excelling in maths, science, music, or art

Over or Under-Sensitivity to Light, Sound, Taste or Touch

Autistic people may experience over or under-sensitivity to sounds, touch, tastes, smells, light, colours, temperatures or pain. For example, they may find certain background noises such as music in a restaurant which other people ignore or block out unbearably loud or distracting sound. This can cause anxiety and even physical pain.

Many autistic people prefer not to hug due to discomfort, which can be misinterpreted as being cold or aloof. Many autistic people avoid everyday situations because of their sensitivity issues. Schools, workplaces and shopping centres can be particularly overwhelming and cause sensory overload. There are many simple adjustments that can be made to make environments more *Autism-friendly*.

Highly Focused Interests or Hobbies

Many autistic people have intense and highly focused interests, often from a fairly young age. These can change over time and can be lifelong. Autistic people become experts in their special interests and often enjoy sharing their knowledge. A stereotypical example are trains. Greta Thunberg's intense interest, for example, is protecting the environment.

Autistic people gain huge amounts of pleasure from pursuing their interests and sees them as fundamental to their wellbeing and happiness. Being highly focused helps many autistic people do well academically and in the workplace, but they can also become engrossed in particular topics or activities that they neglect other aspects of their lives.

Meltdowns and Shutdowns
When everything becomes too much for an autistic person, they can go into meltdown or shutdown. These are very intense and exhausting experiences. A meltdown happens when someone becomes completely overwhelmed by their current situation and temporarily loses behavioural control.

This loss of control can be verbal (e.g., shouting, screaming, crying) or physical (e.g., kicking, lashing out, biting). Meltdowns in children are often mistaken for temper tantrums and parents with autistic children often experience hurtful comments and judgmental looks from less understanding members of the public.

A shutdown appears less intense to the outside world but can be equally debilitating. Shutdowns are also a response to being overwhelmed, but may appear more passive - e.g., an autistic person going quiet or switching off.

One autistic woman described having a shutdown as;

"Just as frustrating as a meltdown because of not being able to figure out how to react to what I want, or not being able to react at all; there isn't any 'figuring out' because the mind feels like it's past the state of being able to interpret."

Causes and Risk Factors
Researchers don't know the primary causes of ASD, but studies suggest that a person's genes can act together with aspects of their environment to affect development in ways that lead to ASD. Some factors associated with an increased likelihood of developing ASD consists of:
- Having a sibling with ASD
- Having older parents
- Having certain genetic conditions (such as down-syndrome or Fragile X syndrome)
- Having a very low birth weight

Diagnosis in Young Children
Diagnosis in young children is often a two-stage process:

Stage 1: General Developmental Screening During Well-Child Check-Ups
Every child should receive well-child check-ups with a paediatrician or an early childhood health care provider. The American Academy of Paediatrics recommends that all children should receive screening for developmental delays between 9-18 months and 24-30 months with specific autism screenings at 18 and 24 months. A child may receive additional screening if they are at high risk for ASD or developmental problems.

Considering caregivers' experiences and concerns is an important part of the screening process for young children. The health care provider may ask questions about the child's behaviour and evaluate those answers with information from ASD screening tools and clinical observations of the child. Read more about screening instruments on the *Centres for Disease Control and Prevention (CDC) website*. If a child shows developmental differences in behaviour or functioning during the screening process, the health care provider may refer the child for additional evaluation.

Stage 2: Additional Diagnostic Evaluation
It's important to accurately detect and diagnose children with ASD on time as this will shed light on their unique strengths and challenges. Early detection also helps caregivers determine which services, educational programs, and behavioural therapies are most likely to be helpful for their child.

A team of healthcare providers that've experienced diagnosing ASD will conduct the diagnostic evaluation. This team may include child neurologists, developmental paediatricians, speech-language pathologists, child psychologists, psychiatrists, educational specialists, and occupational therapists. The diagnostic evaluation is likely to include:

- Medical and neurological examinations
- Assessment of the child's cognitive abilities
- Assessment of the child's language abilities
- Observation of the child's behaviour
- An in-depth conversation with caregivers about the child's behaviour and development
- Assessment of age-appropriate skills needed to complete daily activities independently, such as eating, dressing, and toileting

Because ASD is a complex disorder that occurs with other illnesses or learning disorders, the comprehensive evaluation may include:

- Blood tests
- Hearing test

The outcome of the evaluation may result in a formal diagnosis and recommendations for treatment.

Treatments and Therapies
Treatment for ASD should begin as soon as possible after diagnosis. Early treatment for ASD is important as proper care and services can reduce individuals' difficulties while helping them learn new skills and build on their strengths. People with ASD may face a wide range of issues, which means there's no single best treatment for ASD. Working closely with a health care provider is an important part of finding the right combination of treatment and services.

Medication
A healthcare provider may prescribe medication to treat specific symptoms. With medication, a person with ASD may have fewer problems with:

- Irritability
- Aggression
- Repetitive behaviour
- Hyperactivity
- Attention problems

- Anxiety and depression

Behavioural, psychological, and educational interventions
People with Autism are referred to a health care provider specialising in providing behavioural, psychological, educational, or skill-building interventions. These programs are highly structured and intensive and involve caregivers, siblings, and other family members. These programs help people with ASD in the following categories:

- Learn social, communication, and language skills
- Reduce behaviours that interfere with daily functioning
- Increase or build upon strengths
- Learn life skills necessary for living independently

Many services, programs, and other resources are available to help people with Autism. Here are some tips for finding these additional services:

- Contact your health care provider, local health department, school, or autism advocacy group to learn about special programs or local resources.
- Find an autism support group. Sharing information and experiences can help people with ASD and their caregivers learn about treatment options and ASD-related programs.
- Record conversations and meetings with healthcare providers and teachers. This information helps when it's time to decide what programs and services are appropriate.
- Keep copies of healthcare reports and evaluations. This information may help people with ASD qualify for special programs.

In order to get a better understanding of Autism and find hope, I searched on the internet for answers on how Autism affects individuals over the world and came across a list of famous autistic people and their professions:

Famous People with Autism
- Dan Aykroyd – Comedic Actor
- Hans Christian Andersen – Children's Author
- Benjamin Banneker – African American almanac author, surveyor, naturalist, and farmer
- Susan Boyle – Singer
- Tim Burton – Movie Director
- Lewis Carroll – Author of 'Alice in Wonderland'
- Henry Cavendish – Scientist
- Charles Darwin – Naturalist, Geologist, and Biologist
- Emily Dickinson – Poet
- Paul Dirac – Physicist
- Albert Einstein – Scientist & Mathematician
- Bobby Fischer – Chess Grandmaster
- Bill Gates – Co-founder of the Microsoft Corporation
- Temple Grandin – Animal Scientist
- Daryl Hannah – Actress & Environmental Activist
- Thomas Jefferson – Early American Politician
- Steve Jobs – Former CEO of Apple
- Stanley Kubrick – Film Director
- Barbara McClintock – Scientist and Cytogeneticist
- Michelangelo – Sculptor, Painter, Architect, Poet
- Wolfgang Amadeus Mozart – Classical Composer
- Sir Isaac Newton – Mathematician, Astronomer, & Physicist
- Jerry Seinfeld – Comedian
- Satoshi Tajiri – Creator of Nintendo's Pokémon
- Nikola Tesla – Inventor
- Andy Warhol – Artist
- Ludwig Wittgenstein – Philosopher
- William Butler Yeats – Poet

Despite the challenges associated with the identification of autism spectrum disorder, the above list of names are to inspire those who have family members that are in those categories. Somewhere amidst all this, Ivana and Jane are believed to have the SFNX gene mutation, a rare mitochondrial disease.

My Journey with Twin Angels

We've been informed by consultants that only two children worldwide have been diagnosed with this condition and live in Italy with their parents.

Mitochondrial disease or *mito* is the term given to a group of medical disorders caused by mutations in mitochondria; the tiny organelles that are present in nearly every cell in our bodies and which generate around 90% of the energy we need to live. Cells can't function properly without healthy mitochondria and for this reason, the consequences can be serious when they fail.

Mitochondrial diseases affect people in multiple ways, depending on which cells are affected. This can make the condition hard to diagnose as symptoms often resemble those of other serious illnesses. For example, a person with mitochondrial disease may suffer from seizures, fatigue, vision, hearing loss, cognitive disabilities, respiratory problems or poor growth. In addition, any of the body's organs and systems can be affected including the brain, heart, lungs, gut, liver and skin.

Mitochondrial disease occurs when our mitochondria can't provide the energy our cells need to work correctly. Without the right amount of energy, cells can't do their job and stop performing. If a lot of Mitochondria in the body are affected, mitochondrial disease can be very serious and often fatal.

Each affected individual has different symptoms and severity of the condition because a different combination of their mitochondria is working within each cell. Each person might have different cells in the body that are affected. Mitochondrial disease isn't a single disease, but a collection of conditions. The underlying genetic cause may be different, but will result in the inability of the mitochondria to produce the right amount of energy which causes the disease.

Some types of mitochondrial disease impacts one organ and others, multiple organs. There are times when particular organs and body systems are affected in a recognisable pattern, and these have been given syndrome names such as Alpers's, Leigh's disease, MELAS or MERRF; to name a few.

Mitochondrial disease is also classified by the specific complex of the respiratory chain that they affect, e.g., Complex I. This new diagnosis shook me to the core. It was a confusing as well as bewildering time, and I couldn't help but start questioning God. I felt a grief beyond words, as if a loved one had passed away, but my girls were very much alive.

The feelings of grief don't come in a clear pattern as some people seem to think. Elisabeth Kübler-Ross first articulated the stages of grief as denial, shock, anger, depression, sorrow and finally, acceptance and coping. Kübler-Ross developed her model to describe people with terminal illness facing their own death, but it was soon adapted as a way of thinking about grief in general.

The Five Stages of Grief

Denial
Feeling numb is common in the early days after a bereavement. Some people carry on as if nothing happened. Even if we know that someone has died, it can be hard to believe that someone important isn't coming back. It's also very common to feel the presence of someone who has died, hear their voice or even see them.

Anger
Anger is a completely natural emotion and very natural after someone dies. Death can seem cruel and unfair, especially when you feel someone died before their time or you had plans for the future together. It's also common to feel angry towards the person who has died, or angry at ourselves for things we did or didn't do before their death.

Bargaining
When we are in pain, it's sometimes hard to accept that there's nothing we can do to change things. Bargaining is when we start to make deals with ourselves, or perhaps with God. We want to believe that we'll feel better if we act in particular ways. It's also common to find ourselves going over things that happened in the past and

asking many 'what if' questions, wishing we could go back and change things in the hope things could turn out differently.

Depression
We often think of sadness and longing when we think about grief. This pain can be very intense as it comes in waves over many months or years. Life can feel like it no longer holds any meaning, which can be scary.

Acceptance
Grief comes in waves and feels like nothing will ever be right again, but gradually, most people find that the pain eases, and it's possible to accept what has happened. We may never 'get over the death of someone precious, but we can learn to live again while keeping the memories of those we've lost close to us.

These five stages – denial, anger, bargaining, depression and acceptance are often talked about as if they happen in the exact order, moving from one stage to the other, but this isn't often the case.

Unfortunately, very few people who use these terms understand that we are all individuals and react to things differently. Kübler-Ross in her writing makes it clear that the stages are non-linear. People can experience these aspects of grief at different times, and they do not happen in one particular order. You might not experience all of the stages and may find feelings quite different depending on the challenges you encounter.

Research states that a child with a mitochondrial disease may also have an autism spectrum disorder. When a child has both Autism and a mitochondrial disease, they may have other problems including epilepsy, problems with muscle tone, and/or movement disorders. More research is needed to determine how common it is for people to have Autism and a mitochondrial disorder.

At this current moment in time, it seems rare. I cannot help but question myself daily if I am doing all I can for my Angels. Whilst some people get it, others don't understand that our lives are complicated enough, having the extra responsibility of raising children who require *around-the-clock care*.

My emotions are nearly always in turmoil, and grief hits me unawares, especially when I watch a sad movie or documentary and, at times, in the park when I'm supposed to be having fun and spending quality time with my family. My heart and soul grieved for my imperfect family, and I wept for my childhood dream that was not to be.

The girls were happy and content in their world, but as a mother, I struggled to let go of the dreams I had created during my childhood of the perfect family and home to recreate a new dream. I knew that although it was difficult for me as a mother to accept that my angels were struggling, and that they would require constant care for the rest of their lives, I also came to understand that when seeking open doors for help, resources and a prosperous future for them, it was essential to accept the news so I could find ways to enable them to thrive.

Seizures
The first night Ivana suffered a seizure, I felt as though my chest was being stabbed with sharp objects. It was an intense pain I had never experienced in my life, ever! I had only ever witnessed someone having a seizure once when I worked in an arcade and started to cry and scream. I had no idea what was happening, and my loud sobs came from deep within my soul. As time passed, to my utter shock and dismay, Jane also started having seizures. I felt that God had forsaken me. I was lost, alone and utterly confused.

A grief and constant doom overwhelmed me. One night, I stood by my bedroom window looking out into the pouring rain. Although I knew I wasn't meant to, I started questioning God all over again; *"Why are my babies ill, Lord? Why did they have to be autistic, epileptic and have a rare genetic condition? Why did these innocent beautiful angels have not one, but multiple health conditions? Why could they not be normal?"*

My Journey with Twin Angels

As these myriad thoughts were rushing through my head, raindrops trickled down the window pane in unison with my tears, which had become unstoppable by this time. When the seizures initially started, we thought they were febrile convulsions, which are fits that can happen when a child has a fever; however, due to their frequency, we had to undergo various hospital trips, tests and EEG scans. To our utter dismay, both were eventually diagnosed with epilepsy.

Since that first seizure, everything has been different within the household. I am anxious and constantly on high alert, which makes it difficult to switch off from the day's events and get good quality sleep at night. Fear would grip me as it gets dark, as these episodes mostly happen in their sleep. Although rare, there are sometimes seizures during the day. As these episodes occur without warning, our precious angels can never be left alone.

As a mother, I want to be able to protect them from all kinds of pain and illnesses and would do anything in my power to stop these seizures and their impact on my little angels, but the fact of the matter is, I can't. Night after night, as we put them to bed, we pray for a peaceful and uninterrupted sleep, free of seizures. So far, despite praying these same prayers for years, we are still waiting on God to answer our prayers.

But just like Jane, who keeps repeating and asking for what she wants over and over until she gets it, we will also keep asking God and trusting in His ultimate timing of making all things beautiful. For the last few years, we have been trying out different medications, all with their side effects. As a result of these seizures, the girls have experienced a lack of appetite leading to extreme weight loss and frequent trembling.

Epilepsy
Epilepsy is a neurological disorder that affects the central nervous system. It causes seizures that range from mild to severe. Anyone may have an unexplained seizure once in a lifetime. It's also possible to have one that is provoked by an illness or injury, but a diagnosis of epilepsy means having two or more unprovoked seizures.

My Journey with Twin Angels

According to research, some people with epilepsy can control their seizures with medication. Another fraction is under surgery, however, there are others who must live with drug-resistant epilepsy. Seizures have affected the lives of my precious angels and the entire family.

The seizures and consequences affect every caregiver's world, physical health, emotional health, psychological health, social relationships, education, employment, finances, and the future. These multiple effects often result in stress and anxiety. Caring for Ivana and Jane and watching them in distress can feel like living in a constant state of danger.

Just the thought that there would be another seizure, but not knowing when that would happen is enough to get me in a distressed state. *"What if something different happens this time? What if the seizures go on for too long? What if they choke and stop breathing?"*

Epilepsy did not affect just one person in the family. It affected all of us, and I believe it hit me the hardest as a mum. Even though you know it's not your fault, the decisions you must make while parenting a child with epilepsy are never easy. You will never understand the decisions one has to make that aren't easy unless you parent a child with this disorder.

The countless appointments with doctors, consultants and specialists have been daunting. Constant thoughts such as; "Will a keto or gluten-free diet stop the seizures? Can we use CBD oil or a supplement that works? Do we listen to the doctors and put our girls on medication for the rest of their lives?"

The constant questions that raced through my mind daily were exhausting and left me with very little energy to do anything else. Medicating your child with anticonvulsant drugs is one of the most difficult and, simultaneously, one of the easiest decisions one will ever have to make. For our angels, we resisted medication as long as we could.

Chris and I conducted a significant amount of research about the side effects of the medications used to control epilepsy and found, without exception, that they are horrendous. They are all drugs that affect your brain function to some degree (after all, epilepsy is a neurological disorder). So, we resisted medicating our angels, as their seizures were sporadic and, we believed, tolerable. In short, we were in denial.

Having a child with epilepsy means dealing with parenting issues such as:

- Not being able to switch off and have a good night's sleep because you're worried that a seizure could happen
- Feeling as if you have no control – and that is the truth because we don't. Seizures happen without warning
- The helplessness you feel when seeing your loved one having a seizure
- Watching your child exhausted from a seizure, sleeping for the entire time (which, in our case, causes even more anxiety)
- The powerful love you have for your child and the heartbreak of seeing them suffering and in so much pain

Children with Epilepsy: Tips for Parents
We only want the best for our children, so when some family members are diagnosed with epilepsy, it can be an incredibly emotional and stressful experience for everyone.

"However, despite the risk of seizures and other health concerns, there are steps you can take to help your child with epilepsy and live a normal, healthy, happy life" says Jules E.C. Constantinou, M.D; a Henry Ford neurologist who specialises in paediatric epilepsy.

Get an accurate diagnosis
Diagnosing epilepsy in children poses different challenges than in adults. Depending on the type and severity of a child's epilepsy, the symptoms of certain seizure types may appear as harmless daydreaming – the kind of outward absentmindedness we think of

as common in children. Your child's care team will conduct several medical exams, including an EEG and MRI scans. To provide more information and help develop a more effective treatment plan, you may also be asked to take detailed notes or even a video of your child during a seizure.

The goal is to achieve a seizure-free state, when possible, to minimise the medication side effects, and to enhance the quality of life for your child and family. Monitor your child's medicine. *"Not all children are placed on anti-epileptic medication, a decision that is made in consultation with your child's paediatrician and neurologist,"* Dr Constantinou says.

If your child is placed on epilepsy medication, some questions to ask include:

- How often should they take the medication?
- Should they take it at the same time each day?
- What should I do if they forget to take it?
- Are there any potential side effects?

Make sure your child's school or nursery knows about the epilepsy medication and that arrangements are made to take it at school. You'll also want to educate caregivers about seizure first aid.

Avoid known seizure triggers
Monitor your child's daily activities and write down any seizure triggers. Every child with epilepsy is different, but some common triggers include:

- Stress
- Missed medication
- Lack of sleep
- Infrequently flashing lights

It is important to know that most children with epilepsy have no issue watching TV, viewing computer screens or playing video games.

My Journey with Twin Angels

Recognise the warning signs of a seizure

There are many kinds of seizures with varying degrees of severity and warning signs. These warning signs may include:

- Excessive staring
- Jerking or twitching movements
- Periods of rapid eye blinking
- Stiffening of the body and extremities
- Shallow or accelerated breathing or breathing stops
- Loss of bowel or bladder control
- Not responding to noise or words
- Appearing hazy or confused
- Loss of consciousness
- Excessive nodding or head swaying

"Our children look to us for cues on how to act, and this is even more true for a child with epilepsy who may struggle to cope," says Dr Constantinou. Stay positive and avoid discussing any financial burdens your child's epilepsy places on you or your family. A positive attitude can tremendously affect your child's mood and overall outlook on his or her epilepsy.

Watch for changes in behaviour or mood

For some children, having epilepsy and taking anti-epileptic drugs may affect their behaviour or mood. If you notice any of the following, consult with your child's care team:

- Learning problems or trouble in school
- Irritability
- Withdrawing from friends and family
- Eating less
- Negative statements
- Trouble sleeping

Demystify epilepsy

Encouraging your child to talk about epilepsy may help them feel better. In addition, discuss seizures and epilepsy openly with your child and family. Make sure everyone understands as much about seizures as possible and can assist in an emergency. The Epilepsy Society provides wonderful resources for children and their families to help facilitate this conversation.

Encourage normal activities

Let your child be a child. Please encourage your child to have as much social interaction with other children as possible and to participate in the activities approved by their paediatrician and neurologist. Focus on the things that your child can do and encourage them to be active participants in life. Having epilepsy may create some restrictions, but in general, your child should be able to take part in most activities.

Recognise that your child's epilepsy could change over time

In many cases, children outgrow their epilepsy as they enter their teens. If your child is taking epilepsy medication and has been seizure-free for several years, your child's care team may suggest slowly stopping the medication.

Take time for yourself

"As the parent or caretaker of a child with epilepsy, you make all the difference. Allow yourself time away from your many responsibilities to help avoid caregiver burnout which affects both you and your child," Dr. Constantinou says. Some articles state that epilepsy can be treated, and precautions can control seizures and minimise injuries.

However, most people with epilepsy live long and normal lives, including these celebrities. Read below what these 12 famous people with epilepsy have to say about their condition and be inspired by their bravery:

Lil Wayne

Rap superstar Lil Wayne recently came clean about the condition he dealt with for much of his life. In 2013, he was hospitalised when he had a series of seizures. They occurred after shooting a music video, and was assumed they were brought on by a busy schedule and lack of sleep. Recalling this frightening time, Wayne said, "No warning, no nothing; I don't feel sick. I get headaches really bad. And the headaches? I didn't get no headaches or nothing." After recovering, Lil Wayne opened up in an interview about having multiple seizures throughout his life.

In talking publicly about his epilepsy and what it feels like to have a seizure, the rapper helps to shed light on the condition for his millions of fans. He also made it a point to let his fans know that epilepsy won't damper his career plans or schedule, saying that his doctor "didn't tell him to do too much that a human doesn't do anyway. Sleep and eat right; that's about it."

Theodore Roosevelt
While the 26th President of the United States was perhaps best known for his conservationist efforts, Theodore Roosevelt also stayed active outdoors in the face of numerous health conditions. Among these were asthma, eye problems, and epileptic seizures. While Roosevelt didn't speak about epilepsy directly because of stigmas and eugenic movements during the time he was alive, he did speak about overcoming the challenges.

He was quoted as saying, "Far better is it to dare mighty things, to win glorious triumphs, even though checkered by failure than to rank with those poor spirits who neither enjoy nor suffer much, because they live in a gray twilight that knows not victory nor defeat." He also said, "Courage is not having the strength to go on; it is going on when you don't have the strength."

Indeed, quotes such as these can inspire anyone, but they may especially inspire those who battle specific challenges, like epilepsy, on a regular basis. Despite his health challenges, Roosevelt was known for being active and was involved in numerous professional pursuits throughout his life.

Danny Glover
He will forever be known for his role in the popular *Lethal Weapon* movies, but Danny Glover also impacts people when he talks about epilepsy. The Academy Award-Winning Actor struggled with epilepsy and seizures as a child. Like many people with epilepsy, he outgrew the disorder. Glover attributes part of his success by being

able to recognise the warning signs of seizures after his first one at the age of 15. He said, "Eventually, I could recognise it happening. Each time it got a bit stronger and the symptoms began to diminish to the point where I was ready to go on stage."

Today, Glover works to bring awareness to epilepsy by supporting the Epilepsy Foundation. He contributes to the organisation's programs for children and volunteers his time speaking about epilepsy and bringing awareness to the issue.

Jason Snelling

Former Atlanta Falcons running back; Jason Snelling is another important supporter of the Epilepsy Foundation. He was diagnosed with epilepsy in college. With treatment, he was able to continue his football career and become a successful professional athlete. Snelling has been outspoken about his condition particularly the stigmas and difficulties surrounding the diagnosis.

In an interview, he said that it took a long time for the doctors to diagnose him because not all seizures are due to epilepsy; it could have been a seizure disorder that was caused by something else:

"In my case, it did turn out to be epilepsy," he says. Furthermore, he offers advice on fear and stigma: "You know, there's a big fear factor about having seizures in public, or maybe having one in front of other people, and I like to tell people not to worry so much about that. Epilepsy can be managed and you can go on and do whatever you want to do. I was able to fight my fears and overcome a lot of things; having epilepsy has actually built my character."

Today, Snelling works with the Epilepsy Foundation to bring awareness to the condition. He reaches out to others by speaking out about his own experiences. He also works with the Foundation's African American initiative, *Know the Difference*. Snelling's outreach is helping to bring awareness and funding to this important cause.

My Journey with Twin Angels

Neil Young

Legendary singer-songwriter; Neil Young has long lived with epilepsy. He also has a daughter who inherited the condition. In his memoir, *Waging Heavy Peace*, he writes about his epilepsy and other medical conditions and describes a related medical procedure he underwent years ago. Now banned, the procedure was painful and didn't help his condition. He says, "It has to do with having a radioactive dye injected into your nervous system; basically, into your back, so it goes right into your nervous system. They usually get some bubbles of air and stuff in there too, so when those go through your brain, it's excruciating."

Today, he helps young lives with controlled epilepsy and also helps his daughter to manage her condition.

Susan Boyle

The woman who made waves on *Britain's Got Talent* with her lovely voice has also opened up about having epilepsy. The unlikely star struggled with the condition throughout her childhood. In recalling those struggles, she said: "At school, I used to faint a lot. It's something I've never talked about. I had epilepsy. People in the public eye don't have things like that. All through my childhood they'd say epilepsy is to do with mental function. And now I realise it's not. I was up against all those barriers. It wasn't easy."

Boyle talked openly about her disability and how it held her back. Adults told her that the seizures were due to a mental defect, and for years she believed them. By talking about her struggles, Boyle helps to shine a light on children who may experience complex emotions because of epilepsy.

Prince

Prince; the legendary performer and Grammy Award-Winner first talked about his childhood battle with epilepsy publicly back in 2009. He described being made fun of in school and having supportive parents who weren't sure how to cope with his disorder. He told People Magazine this statement: "My mother told me one day, I walked in to her and said, 'Mom, I'm not going to be sick anymore!' She said 'Why?' I replied, 'Because an angel told me so.' Now, I don't remember saying it, that's just what she told me."

However, the experiences shaped his career and success. Prince explained that the teasing from his classmates forced him to be confident and develop a unique style and persona that helped make him famous. He continues: "Early in my career, I tried to compensate by being as flashy and noisy as I could." The late singer opened up about his epilepsy to further inspire his fans.

Chanda Gunn

Athletes with epilepsy are particularly great at inspiring others to succeed in the face of a physical disability. Among some of the most inspiring is Chanda Gunn; the goalie for the 2006 women's US Olympic ice hockey team. Diagnosed at the age of 9, Chanda was already an avid athlete. When she was forced to give up swimming and surfing, she took up hockey and never looked back.

For Gunn, it's important to let other people with epilepsy know that their condition shouldn't hold them back from their dreams. While ice hockey might be considered dangerous for people with epilepsy, Gunn demonstrates that anything is possible.

On the epilepsy.com website, she writes: *"There's no reason why a person with epilepsy can't play sports or pursue their dreams."* Although she was afraid of the sport, she's now famous for playing and further says, "I've learned to live with it; the fear of the unknown, because I want to really live life, and for me, that means playing ice hockey."

Today, Gunn is one of the most successful women in US hockey and is a spokeswoman for the Epilepsy Therapy Project.

Chapter FIVE

-

Breaking Point

The strongest people are not those who show strength in front of us, but those who win battles we know nothing about.

Author unknown.

Breaking the news of the girls' diagnosis and health challenges to a few friends and family wasn't easy as I'd hoped. Some didn't understand fully what autism was and still don't fully grasp it, and I don't blame them. Unless you've lived a day in the shoes of an autism mum, it is difficult to understand what we go through daily.

I will never forget the day a family member asked me during my late father's memorial after seeing the girls for the first time; "Gee, what about these children?" in our local dialect. The only way I could translate her question was; "Where are these children from, and what is wrong is them?"

She began to offer advice I knew I could never implement in caring for my angels. I wasn't able to put it to use, no matter how well-meaning it sounded at the time. For me, autism has no routine. We pray for peace and calmness; however, we must also be prepared to deal with whatever is presented to us daily. This lecture made me realise that my family, friends and loved ones are essential support systems, and I had to be patient and play my part in getting them to understand exactly what we were dealing with.

As a special needs mum, I can never blame anyone for this, and as our children get older, we can't participate in the same activities that others partake in. However, while our lives revolve around doctors, procedures, and therapists, most parents can pursue various fun activities with their children.

My Journey with Twin Angels

Maintaining relationships hasn't been easy, as there aren't enough hours to go out and meet friends for coffee or dinner. It's hard and takes a lot of effort to maintain friendships with people who don't share the same challenges as we do. However, maintaining friendships with other families that can relate are much more effortless.

It's a fact, and although it's sad, it is what it is. I am very blessed in my journey as we have friends who've supported and stood with us. Even when they don't know what to do or how to comfort us, they stay on the side lines praying and encouraging us.

When it came to finding babysitters so that Chris and I could go out for dinner every now and then or spend quality time together, we always had some challenges. When looking for nannies and/or carers, we had to consider the carers' ability to understand and cope with our girls who depend entirely on us. The questions I had in my mind were:

- Would they be comfortable and empathetic that one or both of them may have a seizure at any time?
- Can these carers recognise when our girls are overstimulated and about to have a meltdown if they don't intervene?

We had a few carers for a short while and one of them couldn't tell us what she'd do if the girls were to have an episode. I'll be honest; the idea of babysitting our Angels terrifies most people. I get it as it can be frightening not knowing what to do amid a crisis, should one happen. This is like foreign territory if it's not your everyday life.

It's intimidating, and I acknowledge that, as I find these episodes frightening myself. Nonetheless, for us as parents, it's also difficult to let go completely and allow other people to look after our sick children, and this is another hard and sad reality which keeps us isolated from the world.

One summertime, we went to a friend's house for a birthday BBQ. The sun was out and we were looking forward to spending the day with friends we had not seen for quite some time. There were lots of people who had gathered after church to join in the celebrations. About an hour after we arrived, I was busy helping out in the kitchen when an elderly lady approached me angrily from the garden and had a go at me because Ivana had hit her grandchild. She told me I had to keep my children in check when going out in public.

Later, it was explained that Ivana didn't know what she was doing, as she was socially unaware of anything happening around her. She was autistic and visually impaired and would often lash out if she thought anyone or anything was coming too close. The woman was apologetic after this, but the harm had already been done.

We took the girls from the party to a nearby park away from all the other children. Once we were safely in the park, I was faced with the stark reality of the future, and the voice that emerged from me after thinking through what had just happened was an agonised deep cry from my heart. The grief that followed was a relentless roller coaster.

Holiday decisions for my family and many others are quite different and not to be taken lightly. We must think through all the fine details, including proximity to hospitals, noise levels, duration of the drive, flight times etc. Although holidays are supposed to be a time of relaxation and unwinding, this never happens for us as a family. Switching off is tough; we all remain full-time carers even while on holiday! For me, the thought of taking the girls to different environments increases my anxiety levels. It's much easier to remain at home with them in an environment in my control.

Once, whilst searching for an autism-friendly holiday, I came across a chateau in the South of France. It was described as the 17th Century Farmhouse, tranquil and pretty, set in a lovely mature enclosed garden, ideal for families and children with additional needs. They were also registered on the National Autistic Service Directory for providing autistic-friendly accommodation.

I was so glad to have found a location which catered for my family's needs and quickly sent an email to enquire about their availability. I received a response from one of the owners who was a lovely lady.

My Journey with Twin Angels

We then built a genuine online friendship and were emailing each other back and forth to arrange our getaway.

The arrangements had been made and we embarked on our long journey to the South of France. Upon arriving at the location, what we saw was nothing like the photos the Internet portrayed. The gilt was quite a distance from the main amenities and attractions; the gardens were overgrown and the swimming pool looked like it hadn't been cleaned in months.

We were met at the entrance by a cleaner and I went on to say that I'd been corresponding with the owner. As soon as I mentioned the lady's name, the cleaner's face fell and became somewhat downcast. She announced that the lady passed away a few weeks before our arrival. This saddened me greatly as it felt like I had made a new friend through our exchange of emails. I endured a grieving phase for a friend I'd never met.

To our utter dismay, the accommodation itself didn't look tidy; the gilt was unbearably hot and the mattresses had mites on it. Our first night was unbearable; we had to bring the mattresses out into the main area and leave the front door open to get some air. Ivana suffered multiple seizures that night and the following morning, we met the husband of the deceased owner.

We requested fans for the property but knowing that he was grieving the loss of his wife, we were mindful not to make any rash complaints. Instead, we decided that we were already far away from home so that we would make the best of a horrible situation.

Needless to say, this was the worst holiday of our lives, and we haven't attempted to go on another break from home since then. The furthest we've been to is Scotland where we found a fantastic property run by a wonderful couple. I often describe Sandford as my happy place set in the glorious Fife countryside; it helps me to pause, take a break, reflect and recharge my batteries.

Another area we struggled with was finding a church where we could worship each Sunday. The various churches we've visited didn't have the resources and staff to look after Ivana and Jane. After months of trying different churches, we finally found a local church who were happy to look after the girls, so we could join the main church. After a couple of weeks, as we went to drop the girls one Sunday, the lady in charge said that one parent had to stay with them, so we agreed. Chris stayed while I went to fellowship with the main congregation.

This continued for a few more weeks; Chris and I would take turns joining the services. One Sunday, however, a volunteer informed us that the normal children were about to watch a movie, so they couldn't take care of our girls that day. I grieved, and it was a deep one as I recounted the Bible verse that children are a gift from the Lord, a reward from Him.

Unfortunately, the church; the one place I thought we could find solace and support, was rejecting our babies. Feeling extremely sad and disappointed, we took our precious girls away, never returned, and stopped attending church afterwards.

Despite some of the negative experiences I endured, I've always believed that God gave me Ivana and Jane for a reason. In addition to caring for them, He entrusted me to raise awareness and help other mothers in a similar place. As a result, I believe my life will continue to be a testimony to others.

With this in mind, I set up the Ivana Jane Foundation to encourage and assist families dealing with children and additional needs within the African community. The Ivana Jane Foundation was launched in the City of London in July 2013, and we were extremely overwhelmed by the support of family and friends. It was a beautiful evening, and I was confident that the vision was so clear-cut I could just run with it. How wrong I was!

Shortly after the launch, I began to experience helplessness and grieve my parents all over again. I missed them and wished they were there to guide me and offer words of comfort during my difficult times. I missed having them as my safe space where I could run to. I kept pushing myself out and trying to hide my fears and anxieties but ended up feeling worse. Pain and sorrow became my identity as I struggled to deal with the medical conditions and diagnoses of my loved ones.

Current and historical events started unfolding in my head; things began to fall apart around me, and I could slowly feel myself sinking into a bottomless black pit. Being perceived as a strong woman by almost everyone around me ensured that my friends and family missed all the signs. I've realised that if society perceives you as strong, it's thought that you should be able to deal with whatever happens around you or comes your way.

At first, many didn't ask about my day-to-day struggles, whether I was anxious or scared about the girls' futures. I understood that this was partly because they genuinely did not know what to say or think of ways to help. I tried to reach out to various people but was constantly shut down with words like, "You are a strong woman! You can deal with it!" Others said God gave them to me because I alone can handle it and nothing was wrong with them; they are like every other child and tell me similar things their children do.

With a forced smile, I would scream in my head, *no, they are not!* A part of me wanted to ask the following questions:

- Does your child trash your home during meltdowns?
- Do they get aggressive towards you?
- Do they pull on your hair, hit, bite or scratch you and the rest of the family?
- Do you have to lock other children away and keep them safe while one of them is having a meltdown?

But no, I never ask; it's simply too exhausting to explain. Once, over dinner, on one of the rare occasions that I'd been able to get out for some time, a well-meaning friend tried to offer reassurance about my angels which left me feeling dismissed, deflated and miserable. "Don't worry," she said, "They will be fine. Life could be so much worse! Did you know that Einstein didn't talk until he was 5?"

My Journey with Twin Angels

Ivana and Jane were eight at this time, offering me little hope. I rolled my eyes and thought that life could be better for them. They could have been normal. Instead, many have tried to reassure me that I am unique, which is why God gave me children with disabilities. I know most of these statements come from a place of love; however, it can be extremely tough to feel special when parenting children with additional needs, so although I understand the intent, I still sometimes find a part of me resenting all these well-meaning statements.

During some of my darkest moments, I provided clues about how I felt on particular days. This was usually through my display picture on WhatsApp. One month, I put a picture of teardrops which went unnoticed until one person finally reached out after the third month to see how we were doing and specifically asked about the picture. I realised everyone was busy getting on with their lives, and not many people understood the grief I was dealing with or didn't know the right words to say. Therefore, I resolved never to talk about my pain to anyone. From that day onwards, I suffered in silence.

Gradually, this started affecting my work. I would travel to work at 9.00 am to sit and stare at my PC until 5.00 pm. My work suffered, and cases started piling up. I was caught in a state of depression that I could care less about work. I walked home every night from the station, crying my eyes out. There was a point where my family would see me with red puffy eyes due to the crying.

After work, I would get home, slump onto the sofa and refuse to do anything for the rest of the evening. I was in a zombie-like state existing in a world of my own. They would gather around me, wanting to know what was wrong, but I always said *nothing; I would be fine*. Everybody was grieving differently; gradually, they stopped asking and I was on my own.

Then one fateful night, I had enough. I couldn't take it anymore! Everything around me was going from bad to worse and decided that if I couldn't change the fate of my children, I no longer wanted to live. I wouldn't have to face or deal with what was to come if I weren't alive. That day, a terrible voice kept echoing in my ears as

My Journey with Twin Angels

I struggled to resist feeling broken and forsaken, asking me, "Where is your God now?"

It was around 11.30pm; I remember stepping out of the house through the back door; I took one last look around me, picking up the bottle of painkillers I hid. With tears streaming down my face, I walked from the house to look for a quiet place to end it all. The only person in the house who heard me leave was Kirsten. She started ringing my phone. I just stared at it, and whilst she sent several text messages, I quickly deleted them all.

I was exhausted, fed up and determined not to communicate with her, knowing that I was in pain and what I was about to do to my life. I walked for hours contemplating whether to throw myself in the path of an oncoming car or take the pills; something that would end my life fast.

Eventually, I kept on walking around the little town where we lived and ended up in a park. Curled up on a bench, I sobbed uncontrollably, letting out all the anguish and frustration. I was in pain, broken and convinced that no one could fix me; not even God. At this point, I'd lost all hope. I wailed like a baby, until suddenly, as if in a dream, I saw myself and my family in that same park! Now, this particular park was one where Chris usually took the girls to play as they loved going outdoors so much.

He'd driven us one Sunday after church, and we had fun running around after the girls whilst pushing them on the swings. Suddenly, the image of us running around amidst the laughter was so vivid, and at that very moment, I couldn't understand why I wanted to end my life. I had a beautiful family. It also occurred to me that the pills may not end my life, but could make me end up in hospital with damaged organs or be in a coma; and then what?

With those thoughts, I started pacing up and down in the park. I diligently served God over the years and offered Him my life, but never expected to deal with these difficult circumstances. I cried out in defiance to God; "What did I do to deserve this?!" At that moment, all I could see around me was brokenness. The night was starry with a fresh nightly breeze, but I was despondent and my heart was extremely heavy.

I started walking again, but this time, slower, not knowing where to go or what to do. Eventually, I dropped into the muddy ground of a big tree. As I sat and stared into the darkness, reflecting on the events of the previous years, I began to examine the grass and weeds around it. Different thoughts and concerns about the future of my precious Angels flooded my mind:

- What if my girls wouldn't be able to talk?
- What if other children teased them at school and in the community?
- Will they ever grow out of these seizures?
- What if we get too old to look after them?
- Who will look after my angels and love them the way I do if I was to die now?

It reminded me of a movie I'd watched when I was a teenager called *'Who will love my children?'* The film is about a mother who was battling terminal cancer. She knew the illness would eventually take her away and resolved to do everything in her power to secure her children's future by finding them suitable homes. Even at that young age, I couldn't stop crying throughout the movie. The tears were unbearable.

In a moment of calmness and solitude, it was as though God was talking to me in that still, small voice:

> **"As complicated as life is right now, do not doubt Me, because I am more than capable. I will strengthen you to deal with the problems as they arise. Just be still and know that I am God."**

Even in my darkest moments, God was with me all along. Somehow, in my grief and anguish, I allowed myself to wallow in self-pity and lost sight of God's mercies and mysterious ways. I'd forgotten that all things are possible with Him as He makes all things beautiful in His time. I stood up from where I was sitting on the grass by the tree, wiping my tears. I pushed the bottle of pills firmly back into my pocket and said a prayer of forgiveness whilst on the long journey back home.

I returned Kirsten's call; unsurprisingly, she'd been worried herself. I informed her that I was coming home. That night, I had the strangest dream; I was in an elevator with another person, but I couldn't recall who. Suddenly, the top tilted and as I looked up, I could see the brightest of lights streaming towards me, engulfing me as I stood in the elevator. I suddenly felt a sense of peace and calmness around me; that was the end of my depressive state.

It's been several years since that day, and I am still on my healing journey. I struggled with many questions regarding grief, including my pain, bitterness and anger. However, I believed that someday, God would restore my brokenness and turn my tears into joy. I woke up feeling refreshed, eager to work and start focusing on my neglected cases.

While walking to the kitchen to make myself tea, I bumped into a work colleague. Somehow, we ended up talking about babies and how some were struggling to have children. She looked at me and said, "Gee; you know someone would kill to have your children; enjoy them."

Another realisation hit, and I couldn't help but feel that God sent another angel in the form of my colleague to let me know that it was going to be alright. From that moment onwards, I turned my negative feelings into positivity before they started affecting my self-worth whilst building a heart of gratitude. I began thanking God for making me live to see my girls for their abilities rather than their inabilities. As a distraction, I focused on fundraising events for my secondary school alumni, participated in mini marathons and raised money for charities including the National Autistic Society.

For many parents, learning that their child has an illness, a disability or slow growth is the beginning of a long, agonising, frustrating and painful process. First, you go through a period of mourning, grieving the loss of hopes and dreams you'd planned for your children.

My Journey with Twin Angels

It doesn't matter what illness your child has been diagnosed with; parents will still go through a long, frightening and painful grieving process as they navigate the unknown waters.

According to research, the number of pupils with Special Educational Needs (SEN) increased to 1.49 million pupils in 2022, representing 16.5% of all pupils. Numerous studies have been conducted about the review of grieving the entire family and the experiences due to the loss of the perfect child. Here are some highlights:

- The grieving process for families that have disabled children can last as long as the grieving process for families with children who've passed away

- The negative emotions experienced as part of the grieving process are significant and includes sadness, anger, resentment, shock, denial, anxiety, guilt, shame, depression, disappointment, confusion, self-doubt, humiliation, and any combination thereof

- Every individual goes through stages of grief in their time

- Negative emotions that aren't addressed can lead to alienation, avoidance, withdrawal and isolation for family members

Due to my cultural background, I'd never for once contemplated having children with special needs and was faced with this enormous challenge. One of my immediate reactions was denial; "Was this *really* happening to me, my children, my family?! No; this couldn't!" This turned into anger that it affected almost everyone.

My grief was inexplicable, and I didn't know how to explain or deal with it. I experienced all negative emotions with a mixture of joy, sorrow, pain, and tears. On the outside, I smiled bravely, laughing and pretending that it was all okay, but inside, I was hurting deeply and wanted nothing more than to crawl in bed and hide away from the rest of the world.

Although I'd purposed in my heart that I'd enjoy my angels, no matter the diagnosis or the challenges, it was difficult to do in practice. My girls went to a special primary school in the village, and one Christmas, we went as a family to watch them in a school play. Other children were talking and singing whilst my children sat down quietly observing or occasionally dancing excitedly on stage.

A wave of emotions swept over me, and I burst into tears. I prayed that my angels were the ones singing. I clasped Chris and Khaela's hands so tight that they wondered what was going on with me. Inevitably, Khaela also wept.

Through my tears, I managed to mumble to them that I wished it was my girls who had the power of speech and were singing on stage. Chris turned and said to me, "But they sing!" He explained, "They sing, but they can't say the words, but, eventually, they will." My heart filled with pride and gratitude as my angels danced on stage to the song "I did it my way" by Robbie Williams. Of course, they did it their way, which was a beautiful sight!

Chapter SIX
-
A Childhood Shared

The siblings of special needs' children are pretty special. Accepting and loving from birth, someone who is different mentally, and has a different way of seeing the world, is a beautiful trait.

Sally Phillips.

Throughout my journey, I have found that there are particular groups of people we tend to forget when our lives are wrapped around the children that require special attention. As well as sharing many of their parents' concerns, they also have to deal with their own emotions, most often alone. Siblings spend more time with children with additional needs and are actively involved in caring for them. This is usually in addition to facing their unique trials and challenges.

My beautiful daughters know nothing else besides being helpers and caring for others. Whilst I'm not perfect, I am learning that the feelings and concerns of these siblings must never be ignored. I go through several days of heartache because I am engrossed in dealing with the newest symptoms, medications, and endless consultations with specialists and therapists. This often means that I can't sit down and spend quality time with my girls the way I'd love to.

A few years ago, we went on a family mini break with Khaela and her friend to Norfolk; a beautiful holiday destination ideal for short breaks. They were both 13 years at the time. We had been getting to know the family and were invited around their house a couple of times. They knew about our angels and the difficulties we were experiencing as a family regarding the differing diagnoses. So, it seemed okay when their daughter decided she wanted to spend time with us on holiday.

My Journey with Twin Angels

On a day out, Ivana had a meltdown in the car and pulled her hair. She wouldn't stop crying and called her mother to pick her up. They had a holiday home in Norfolk, and within 20 minutes, her mother was there to pick her up. Without so much as glancing in our direction, she rushed to her daughter, spoke to her to ensure that she was okay, and helped her get in the car. That was the last time the two families talked with each other. Khaela and her friend both attended the same secondary school and haven't spoken since that day. It was an awful experience and I was heartbroken for my daughter.

This experience had a substantial negative impact on Khaela's life. Thankfully, she had a wonderful supportive group of friends who rallied around and supported her during that dreadful time. As for Kirsten, I have no recollection of her friends being invited over during the primary and secondary school years; only inviting one friend home whilst she was at university.

Shortly after this experience, I contacted a friend whose sister had been diagnosed with cerebral palsy at birth. We began discussing the impact of special needs on families. She said, *"I felt completely isolated from my friends and struggled to maintain relationships as none of them had the same responsibilities as I had. They didn't understand what I went through as a young carer."*

She went on to say that despite her difficult childhood as a sibling to a loved one requiring constant care, she felt that it helped her achieve success in many areas of her life. With everything relating to disabilities, each situation is unique. We mustn't generalise this as each sibling reacting to their situations and family dynamics differ. For some siblings, life with autism can be overwhelmingly tricky; for others, it has ups and downs. Some even see their siblings' disabilities as a blessing to shape them into the people they are today.

Isolation is an overall experience among siblings. Many need the opportunity to talk about their feelings and home environment, especially with their parents, as these are complicated subjects. As they go through the years, siblings don't always know how to respond to others' teasing and may feel alone with their conflicting experiences. As a result, many siblings keep their feelings to themselves which eventually builds up over the years; sometimes breeding resentment.

In addition, siblings may have difficulties asking questions for fear of upsetting their parents. The Covid-19 pandemic and lockdown created further isolation and challenges for this group of remarkable people. It's also challenging for parents to talk about what's happening because of their own emotions, as they may be going through a range of pain, denial, and anger which can at times, be a coping mechanism.

Some siblings accept and understand their special needs' brother or sister. Others may feel embarrassed or under pressure to compensate by becoming a 'super child.' When this happens, we must let them have a life of their own. It's easy for your energy and effort to go towards the child requiring additional attention as more time is spent going to therapist appointments and other supportive specialists. Academic issues which form a part of the parenting journey will also have to be dealt with.

Whilst most siblings adjust to living at home and appear to be coping very well, *Contact A Family*; a UK-based charity, suggests that these children seem to thrive when they are given a chance to talk things over, expressing their feelings and opinions. This can help them deal with any difficulties that may arise in the future.

Siblings of special needs children may feel *slighted* at times. If this happens, be assured you're not a bad parent. You're only human. Below are some useful tips from other parents on dealing with everyday issues and solutions:

- ***Limited time and attention for other children?*** Protect your time and spend it with your siblings. For example, bedtime or an outing once a month. Organise short-term care for important events such as Sports Day. Put the needs of siblings first and let them choose what to do

- ***Why them and not me?*** Emphasise that no one is to blame for their brother's or sister's condition. Encourage siblings to see their brother or sister as a person with similarities and differences to theirs

- ***Worry about bringing friends home?*** Talk over how to explain a sibling's condition to friends. Occasionally, invite friends over when the disabled child is away and don't expect siblings to include the disabled child in their play or activities

- ***Stressful situations at home?*** Encourage siblings to develop their own social life. For example, a bedroom door or lock can ensure privacy to prevent damaged possessions

- ***Get professional advice about tasks*** – this includes handling difficult behaviour which siblings can be included

- ***Keep the family's sense of humour going*** – it brings unity and a sense of belonging

Do not hesitate to involve specialist therapists for assessment and treatment if you have concerns regarding your child's behaviour or mental health. Research is, however, limited in the understanding of siblings' lived experiences.

The Glass Children*:* The lived experiences of siblings with a disability or chronic illness are a study and semi-structured interview of 16 siblings who grew up with a chronically ill brother or sister. The study is aimed to address the gap in literature through an in-depth qualitative interview study that examines the lived experiences of siblings. Participants were allowed to reflect on their childhood and adolescent experiences, focusing on their social interactions, relationships, social support and general well-being.

The study uncovered the following themes:

(A) Feelings of invisibility during social interactions

(B) Psychological difficulties due to the internalisation of family roles or life conditions

(C) Experiencing guilt and self-blame for not being able to offer constant support to their brothers or sisters or due to leading independent lives

(D) Issues related to social support such as siblings' inabilities to understand their own needs and the importance of support from family and peer groups in helping them have their experiences validated

Unless you raise a special child, or have a sibling with needs, it is difficult to understand what we go through. The daily struggle is real! It takes perseverance to show up every day. Despite the frustrations, anger, sadness, and other negative feelings they experience, I am proud of my two big girls and love who they are becoming. They've had more responsibilities than their peers; a different kind of life impacted by disability. There's a lot of effort in choosing *kindness* when you are filled with anger, *joy* when you feel defeated, and *hope* when you can't see the light at the end of the tunnel.

I see compassion, kindness, and sensitivity to others' feelings in their interactions. My two beautiful girls are wise beyond their years with hearts full of acceptance, compassion, and a deeper understanding about the value of life. I am confident that God will use their experiences that cause them the most pain to continue developing positive character traits that will be invaluable to them, both now and in the future.

Hence, they will go out into the world and make a difference, not just for Ivana and Jane but for all of us.

Chapter SEVEN
-
Things every parent of children with special needs should know

If you can't run, then walk. If you can't walk, then crawl; but, whatever you do, you have to keep moving forward.

Martin Luther King Jr.

Asking for help from others can be challenging for everyone; however, it's a viable way of making life easier. Remember that you are unable to do all tasks by yourself. Be open minded to delegate tasks and don't be afraid to ask for support. More importantly, accept the help when offered.

Support can come in different forms including having someone to look after the children for a few hours, helping with bath and bedtime routines, tidying up your home, help from professionals to know what actions one must follow next or being able to talk with someone. Whatever form it comes in will make everything easier and achievable than doing it alone.

After our angels were born, most family and friends reacted similarly; there were extreme feelings of sadness which made me feel compelled to comfort them, often at a time when I had no emotional energy to take care of myself. I realised that only a few people understood my journey, so they offered little solace. Many loved ones understood our daily struggles after they visited and saw us in action with our girls.

Most people became speechless and there were feelings of guilt for assuming that we were doing well and coping with the situation. My circle of support now know that when they suspect a friend may be going through tough times, they ask them how they're doing, lend a listening ear, take them out to lunch or dinner, invite them to come and sit for a coffee, and offer any help they can.

One day, as I sat next to my colleague having our early morning catch-up before settling down, she told me that she was in the process of buying a house; however, the process was taking so long. She had to stay at her friend's house for a few weeks while waiting for the completion stage. She turned around and said to me; "I don't want to stay there!" I asked; "Why?" She gave me her reasons, and I responded, "Why ever not?"

As soon as I uttered these words, I was hit with an instant realisation. Indeed, in my life, it's always been hard for me to ask for help. However, others don't hesitate to come and enquire of me when they have something I could help them with. I walked to the vending machine in shock. I couldn't believe I had just told someone to ask for help, especially as this was an area I struggled with. "Ask for help! Me? From whom?! I didn't even have a cleaner!"

Over the years, friends and family had encouraged me to enquire about a cleaner, at least for a monthly deep clean in my home, as I couldn't work a full-time job and do all the house chores at the same time. I resisted this for a few years as I wanted to guard my space with the children and didn't want any activities going on that would be too intrusive for them. However, once I committed to having a deep clean once a month, it made a massive difference in our lives.

Some friends and family members, especially within the Christian community, would chastise me if I said my children weren't okay. Various organisations and Government schemes within the UK assist families with learning difficulties, including supportive schemes and assistance with financial resources.

However, a good few years after Ivana and Jane were born, I was made to assume that as we were praying and believing God for healing, applying for Government assistance meant that I'd accepted that my children did have disabilities; therefore, the devil had won the battle. I was only encouraged to speak words of positivity into my circumstances.

My Journey with Twin Angels

As a result, I leant to stifle my grief and sorrow. Now, if I had to do it all over again, I wouldn't hide my anguish and pretend that everything was okay with my girls and was coping just fine. Instead, I'll tell my friends, family, and anyone who cared to know that I needed extra compassion and kindness. They could do anything to make my life manageable because I needed their help.

I have a small group of incredibly supportive friends and family who understand what we are going through and often go out of their way to be there for us. The thought is comforting as you learn who matters on this journey and who to keep in your life for the good times. I've had some of my loved ones turn up on our doorstep with flowers and food, unannounced ready to sit with us for a few hours. So, we'd sit, talk, cry and laugh. I'd be lost without my fantastic support system!

Some friends have offered to watch the girls for Chris and me to take a break for a couple of hours. Of course, they don't have to do all that, yet they do. I also understand that friendship means different things to people. We have a wonderful mix of people around us from school, colleagues, ex-colleagues, and those we've met on our unique journey. We are each fearfully and wonderfully made; our differences make us all beautiful, and as they say, variety is the spice of life! They've made me understand that they're there for me and that asking for help is a sign of strength, not weakness.

Something I've found helpful is connecting with others who are navigating similar issues as myself. There might not be anyone else with the same symptoms as your children, but there are people with similar challenges. I've never met families with the same diagnoses and challenges as my girls, but being surrounded by a strong network within each diagnosis is a blessing. It took me a long time to connect with others as I didn't want to think about what would happen to my angels in the future.

One day, I met a childhood friend for lunch, and while staring intently at the food on his plate, he asked me, "So Gee, what are your plans for the girls? Have you put anything in place so that Kirsten and Khaela don't suffer, especially financially, in the future?" I looked up at him in shock, and I will be sincere here – until that point, I was living daily with no thoughts about the future. It was all about the here and now.

At that moment, I decided to wake up as a mother and let go of my limiting beliefs to redefine my purpose. I couldn't let being a special needs mum become my identity and push me towards a life of mediocrity. Owning my story and letting go of what I couldn't change shaped my mindset in an empowering way during that time. In the words of Napoleon Hill; "Whatever the mind of man can conceive and believe, it can achieve!" There would be no more settling. My four beautiful girls deserved more!

I sprang into action and was thankful to find many groups on social media. I eventually joined a few on Facebook. Some of these groups share and allow me to ask questions about everyday parenting issues, struggles, resources, various treatments, medications, etc. I have access to tools, knowledge, skills, and networks that provide me insight into making more intelligent decisions about finances and my life.

I've made some costly mistakes along the way, and at the same time, learnt a few lessons. I've found a great deal of support within these communities. I just have to go on my Facebook groups and am immediately reminded that the journey I'm on isn't done in isolation. Joining these groups allows me to realise my goals and connect with like-minded people in supportive communities. But most of all, I've built amazing friendships worldwide.

Have I been hurt by comments that friends and family members have made? Yes, I have. Like when I posted a picture of the girls on Facebook, someone commented, "Look at their eyes." The girls had a severe visible stint due to visual impairment, and I was deeply hurt. I'm sure some of these remarks weren't meant to be hurtful. However, we must find positive people we can trust, educate them on our unique journey and build a strong circle of support.

Acknowledge your feelings

Coming to terms with your child's unique needs can feel like a grieving process. Your hopes and dreams have to be cast out and redefined. These feelings are entirely normal. It's okay to cry. As my angels have a challenging diagnosis and are going through pain, I find myself weeping quite a lot. Many people tend to see crying as a sign of weakness, but it's the natural response to the emotions we experience. Holding up tears isn't healthy, so let them out.

For me, crying is a way of releasing pent-up stress, anger, frustration and grief. It allows me the time to acknowledge those feelings so I can refocus and move on. It's important not to let these feelings consume you, so let it all out and turn your focus back on the positive, enabling you to move forward. You may find it helpful to contact organisations such as Care for the Family, who can put you in touch with another parent in a similar situation to yourself through their befriending scheme.

Self-love and self-care is key

This is a crucial one! As Caregivers, we are always placed in a position of caring for our loved ones. Between all the challenges, doctor's appointments, school meetings, and for some mothers like myself who might be juggling full-time careers, having children with special needs can be exhausting; however, you still need and deserve to be cared for. This can be asking friends or family to bring a meal around, going for a manicure, pedicure, date night, or whatever else you enjoy doing.

Whatever makes you feel special and taken care of, take the time to enjoy it because you are so worth it! As a mum, I struggle with this because I don't have time for myself, but I also understand that if I want to be the best mother, I need time to relax and recharge my batteries.

Have you ever heard the saying, "You can't pour from an empty cup?" Think of your energy as a cup of water; if you constantly pour out your energy (the water) but never refill it, you'll be burnt out and have nothing to give anyone at the end of it all. Do not see taking time out for yourself as selfish – it's essential to take the time to replenish your mind, soul, spirit and body. Find someone you can trust to look after your child and go for coffee with a friend; go for a run, find a hobby, take a long hot bath, go for a massage or spend time with your partner or loved ones.

Here are a few quick tips a group of mothers and I have used throughout the years:

- Permit yourself to take 5-10 minutes each day just for yourself

- Do something you enjoy that brings relaxation (a cup of tea or coffee, read a book, lock yourself in the bathroom and have a long hot soak, or sit and do nothing)

- Use the buddy system – Put the children in their buggies, buddy up with a friend or neighbour and take a walk. The children will benefit from the change of scenery and fresh air and you will feel energised

- Driving – I especially love *me-time* in the car and often, pray, listen to music or my favourite audiobooks

- Exercise – Take long walks and hit the gym, even if it's 10 minutes of cardio or stretching. Just do something and keep moving

- See yourself as a superhero

When you are a mum who looks after children with additional needs, you may not perform those heroic acts as we see in the movies, but your day-to-day responsibilities make you a super mum nonetheless. You administer medication daily and manage situations that a regular parent would think are impossible or can't cope with. You deal with tantrums and meltdowns, holding yourself together while avoiding a tantrum, tears or meltdown yourself. You are a mummy, therapist, nurse, doctor, friend and cheerleader. You are no regular parent. You are mummy, the superhero! Give yourself some credit.

Therapeutic play

Playing with your children will strengthen your relationship with them. Find out what activities your child enjoys so you can collectively join in. Playing is essential for your child's physical, emotional, social and brain development and helps them with their creative skills, imagination and coordination.

In addition, the self-esteem of children with special needs is fragile and easily damaged, and they need us to believe in them and offer consistent encouragement. So be reassuring; celebrate their great personality traits and be proud of who they are. This, in turn, will become a win-win situation for the family.

Make time to enjoy your children

We super mums are constantly busy. However, while everything on your calendar is essential, making time to play, laugh, be silly, and enjoy your children are crucial. Read to them, snuggle with them and engage with them with what's important in their worlds. Create memories at home, in parks, and anything enjoyable outside of the hospital walls, which has become the norm.

You will be obliged to make heart-wrenching decisions

You will have to make painful decisions that hurt your heart but try not to be too hard on yourself and know that you are doing your best. I am guilty of agonising over these types of decisions, whether to stop the girls from having periods which will, in turn, reduce seizures; all this can become overwhelming for me. Talk about your issues and difficulties with others who understand and trust yourself to make the best decision for your child or children.

Make the decision and move on. Once it's made, don't rethink it. It's easier said than done, but it's worth a try! Understand that many life choices you'll make will have no correct answer, just the lesser of the hard and painful wrong decisions. Endeavour to do your best because you will only get it right at times, no matter how many sleepless nights you agonise over handling a situation.

Be kind to yourself

As caregivers, we don't get it right all the time. Yes, you will make mistakes despite having the best intentions. Please understand that you don't need to torture yourself when plans don't go as expected. Remember the most challenging decisions we have to make, whether parenting a child with additional needs has no right or wrong answer.

There is no parenting manual. Whenever you get negative thoughts to be self-critical, resist the urge to be harsh and remind yourself that this line of thinking won't help you or your loved ones. Be kind to yourself; tomorrow is a new day which presents new opportunities to try different approaches that might lead to better solutions.

Being a parent is hard

Being a parent to a child with additional needs is a serious responsibility. Although extremely challenging, it can also be extra rewarding as it makes us mothers extra passionate, which makes life more pleasant. With life's challenges come the rewards. You have to search your heart for the prizes, and though it seems like searching for a needle in a haystack, you will find them if you look for them hard enough.

Parenting a child with additional needs is like running a marathon

There are no breaks for runners trying to win a marathon. In 2005, I watched Paula Radcliffe, a famous British runner stop, squat and relieve herself by the side of a road at the 22-mile mark as she was having severe stomach cramps. I'm sure she had a choice to either stop or continue running in pain. She did what was best for her and went on to win the race.

If you want to stay in the race, you have to eat well and drink lots of water. However, as mothers with special needs children, our marathon will go on for the foreseeable future and beyond! Remember to keep taking small steps forward; stop when you need to and don't lose yourself in the process.

Don't let being the mother of a special needs child create or reshape your identity

Being the parent to a child with special needs form *part* of our identity, but it shouldn't be all of our identity. When you focus your life around your child and their needs, who you are can get lost. So instead, find what you enjoy doing, read a good book, have a glass of wine, partake in a hobby, go and enjoy several shopping activities and schedule out time to have fun with your friends.

Celebrate the little things

Brag about the accomplishments that seem small to others but huge for our children! Our children develop on their own clock; they learn many skills at a later stage; others, they may never master. Therefore, share a first word, sentence, smile, hug; whatever that milestone may be with those who love you and your child.

Do not compare

This is another challenging one for us mothers, but it's worth the effort. All children are different with extra challenges and will grow and develop at their own pace. Comparing siblings, cousins and children in a class or comparing children with the same disability type rarely makes you feel better. Your child is unique and will have strengths and challenges.

Do what makes you comfortable

We all know that mothers will go the extra mile to buy the most fabulous gifts for teachers at school to appreciate all they've done for their children on the last day of term. Some will send party bags for every birthday. If this is you, that's perfectly fine. Unfortunately, I hardly have enough energy to go around and will do what I can, including not over-exerting myself to attend every weekly engagement.

Dedicate time to your marriage

Marriage is hard work, and special needs parenting is additional work. For those who are married or in a relationship, get help and make time for your spouse allowing it not to impact your children in any way.

Trust your instincts

As the primary caregiver, you are the expert for your child. Mothers know their children best. Doctors, teachers and therapists are fantastic resources. Nonetheless, getting a second opinion is reasonable if you don't feel that you're being heard or your child's needs aren't being met. Don't be afraid to fight for your child's needs and what's best for them. While professionals are experts in their chosen fields, you are your child's primary caregiver and expert.

Talk to the following group of people if you require assistance with:

- A paediatrician regarding referrals to specialists

- A child's teacher for additional suggestions to help your child academically

- A pastor, minister, counsellor, or other special needs parent for personal support

- Ensuring other children without special needs are recognised as a young carer and receiving pastoral support at school.

- A spouse or co-parenting partner to brainstorm family solutions

- Friends and family for possible *you-time* to recharge your batteries

Practice gratitude

Writing in a gratitude journal daily helps to increase your overall well-being and happiness. Your journal will help to refocus on the positives in your life and create sacred memories to reflect on as you navigate challenging circumstances you find yourself in. I look back on my old journals and have been moved by moments that meant so much to me. Practising gratitude helps me appreciate the present and see its beauty, even in dark moments. Most of us have busy lives getting caught up with day-to-day challenges.

However, I've come to understand that there's always something to be grateful for, and expressing appreciation eventually changes my outlook for the better. As mothers of children with special needs, we spend our time playing nurse, solving problems, and overcoming obstacles; nonetheless, how often do we take the time out to celebrate the positives? Journaling can be incorporated in your morning or night-time routine; whichever way you see fit. My wellness journal has sections on self-care, activities, thoughts, feelings, hours of sleep and meals.

LeeAnn Karg, Med, (kargacademy.com) offers the following tips for creating success and comfort at home:

Create predictable schedules
Develop a daily and structured schedule simple enough to be adapted to any situation. Endeavour to commit with following the routine, no matter where you are or who you're with. Always remember that sudden changes to routines can cause stress and anxiety. In addition to this, the following successes according to LeeAnn consists of:

- **Structuring everything** – Break down every activity into small and simple steps. Approach every activity one step at a time because they must be approached gradually. Practice every new activity or skill privately before trying it in a social setting

- **Being prepared** – Don't plan any activities without allowing at least a full week for preparation. Make sure you have pictures of people or places you will be visiting. Leave nothing to chance so that nothing will be of a surprise

- **Simplifying your speech** – Give logical and direct explanations by reducing the amount of information you provide to your child in order to increase stimulation from their environments

- **Paying attention** – Be aware of sensory inputs from the environment including noise, temperature, smell, lighting, textures, peoples, animals, etc

- **Employing coping strategies** – Teach specific coping strategies to your child for each anxiety-provoking event and every possible instance of sensory overload. Practice those coping skills every day

- **Being concrete** – Be logical, clear, organised and concise in all communication with your child. State every direction and expectation clearly and follow up with virtual cues and timed verbal reminders

- **Understanding the cause and effect** – Teach your child specific cause-and-effect relationships to help them cope with the unpredictability of social interactions. Learn about social competence and how to teach it to your children

- **Organisation skills** – Teach your child organisational and time management skills so they are able to deal with specific tasks at school and at home

- **Using strengths** – Use your child's strengths to help them with their weaknesses. For example, verbal explanations can clarify visual material and visual demonstrations can enhance verbal instructions

- **Reflection** – Teach your child how to recognise and use non-verbal communication and how to practice it if they can. Teach your child how to recognise their audience's physical and facial reactions to determine whether they are communicating effectively including role-play social interactions in group activities

As I've gone on this journey, I've often asked myself; "Well, if this didn't happen to me but to one of my friends or family, what would I have said to them? How could I have helped them?" I wouldn't know what a proper response should look like, so I asked around and spoke to several parents of children with disabilities. I asked them what they wished people had said to them. Most of the answers I received are also summarised below:

What to say to parents who has a child with additional needs
Reference: Stanley D.Klein, Ph.D and Kim Schive, 2001. Title – You will Dream new Dreams; New York, Kensington Publishing Corp – Pages 88-89.

Learning about the hardships of special needs parents and what they endure is heart-wrenching. It's said that *it takes a village to raise a child*, but for us special needs parents, we require an entire village often to make it through the day! If you know anyone parenting a child with additional needs, don't hesitate to tell them how much of an inspiration they are.

When special needs parents open up to you, the best response you can give is to reassure them they are doing well. Lend a listening ear and be more open to learning about their experiences. Responses like these make a great difference in the life of a special needs parent.

You can also offer to help them with what they need during the week. For example, to pick their child from school, do grocery shopping, cook for the family, buy a self-care item for the parents, and so much more. An additional benefit is to compliment the child and their parents.

I remember a time when Chris and I were holding our twins in the hospital corridors, and almost every passer by commented on their beauty. The words and actions of our family members and friends made a huge impact in our lives after the girls were born.

More support can consist of offering to babysit and learn about the child's disability by reading books about known and unknown diagnoses. Make yourself available and let their families know this. Parents with special needs children don't have time or the energy and often feel they are troubling you and may not have the boldness to ask for assistance.

What <u>not</u> to say to parents of a child with additional needs
Reference: Stanley D.Klein, Ph.D and Kim Schive, 2001. Title – You will dream new dreams; New York, Kensington Publishing Corp – Pages 88-89.

Avoid stereotypical statements such as "They all…" Remember that every person with a disability is unique in their own right. Avoid making statements which convey pity. For example, do not say:

"I'm sorry!"
"What a shame!"
"Poor thing!"
"Life could've been much worse!"

No matter what the diagnosis is, the parent may feel that nothing could be worse than what they're currently dealing with. Avoid any statement that implies to parents or grandparents that it may have been their fault. This is particularly true for children that are diagnosed with autism, attention deficit disorder or speech delays. Don't attempt to rationalise why God allowed this to happen. Avoid statements like "God gives special children special parents."

I've had several conversations around these specific statements, and while I believe God has a purpose for everyone in life, I don't believe in making blank statements without a genuine purpose behind it. We want our children to be better and have normal lives.

Taking care of ourselves
Parenting a child with a disability is about letting go and learning to live with the realities. Yes, I've had to let go of my childhood dreams. I've had to accept that my home may never be decorated as I want it to with expensive gadgets, flowers and scented candles in every corner. If I've learnt anything whilst raising our imperfect angels, it's about taking care of myself.

My Journey with Twin Angels

As a married couple, our journeys are so stressful that we must take care of ourselves and do something that removes the day-to-day stresses. Walking and working out are great ways to relieve stress. I take time out twice a week to go to the gym after work. I also do cardio at home before the working day starts. Sundays are for walking and sightseeing in our idyllic village and spending time with myself by putting money in my sanity bank. I do this to thrive and give back.

To conclude, here are some ways to keep your sanity:

- Exercise often
- Run a lot
- Join and attend book clubs
- Join support groups for parents and carers
- Surround yourself with positive people

Follow your passion
Any mother on this journey will tell you that raising children, managing a household and being a good spouse is tough! Imagine the additional responsibilities of raising an exceptional child; life gets more complex, challenging and frustrating. The definition of success has a different meaning to each of us, and it may take a lot of work to see life with enough time, energy and resources to pursue your dreams. However, this is still possible! Although it may take time, work, effort and structure, journaling and creating a vision board has helped immensely.

Chapter EIGHT

-

Beauty for Ashes

But where we see trash, God sees potential. The Master Artist, with His tender touch, can rework our suffering into a pattern of good.

Tessa Emily Hall.

Towards the end of 2021, during the Covid-19 lockdown, I suffered another setback. The familiar feelings of dread, fear and sorrow returned after discovering a lump in my left breast while on holiday. Although I heard that some breast lumps are benign, this was a frightening and painful experience. I showed Chris the lump, however; we both agreed to keep it to ourselves and not worry the girls.

Pretending I was okay during our time away was particularly tough as I wondered what would happen or who would care for my girls if the lump turned out to be cancerous and I passed away. My mind kept telling me that I had cancer and had difficulty sleeping and keeping these thoughts at bay.

As soon as we returned home, I contacted my doctor, who immediately booked me in for a lump examination. After a physical examination of the breast under my arm, the nurse booked me for further tests, including a mammogram and ultrasound.

The doctor told me a week later that the tests didn't provide enough information about the lump and recommended a biopsy which involved inserting a long needle into the node to collect a tissue sample for testing. Once again, I was terrified, and my faith levels were severely tested during that time. Emotionally drained and in turmoil, I asked God why He'd let me go through this when my life was difficult enough. I cried throughout the entire process.

My Journey with Twin Angels

During the same time, I lost a work colleague. We never met as I'd been working from home during that period and interacted virtually with him. It was a strange period in my life as I began to realise the crux of my problem. I'd never really dealt with anything properly in my life. I came from a loving family with two wonderful brothers: Michael and Felix. Michael was my second daddy. He took me to school, picked me up, ensured I was always okay and that I had a happy childhood.

On the other hand, Felix was the thorn in my side, constantly picking on me and getting me in trouble with our parents, but he fiercely protected and loved me passionately. One day, I came home from school to meet my parents, sitting quietly in the front room with Felix. During the meeting, they announced that Michael had left home and was nowhere to be found. This was in 1987. Fast forward to 2023, Michael hasn't returned to his birth home. Michael, my beloved brother, vanished without a trace.

This experience was troubling and damaging for me. In hindsight, I don't think I dealt adequately with the loss of my big brother. With him and my parents gone, Felix was all I had left. Unfortunately, he was also diagnosed with chronic kidney disease in 2016. As far as I know, my whole existence has been a series of dealing with tragic pain, one after the other, and now I had to deal with a possible cancer diagnosis.

Finally, after an agonising wait, we received the news that the lump was benign. I was thankful to God, but deep down, I was still scared, had self-doubt and spent my whole life trying to deal with challenging issues at the enormous expense of my well-being.

After a long hard day of dealing with meltdowns and tears one Saturday afternoon, I put the girls in the car and went for a long drive. I was engulfed by grief and wanted to drive us into a deep ditch, off a cliff if I could find one, or anything that would end it all for us. I was shocked by my thoughts and burst into tears behind the wheel. I was utterly broken and once again felt so sure that I couldn't be fixed.

My Journey with Twin Angels

Accepting and going into therapy helped me deal with long-standing issues along the long, difficult and exhausting route of self-acceptance. Gradually, I began to look at various issues, including dealing with my grief and the belief system that guided me all these years.

One evening, after I had put the girls to bed, I was on the internet looking for inspiration for mothers who were in the same position as me, parenting children with additional needs and feeling exhausted. I came across the Japanese word "Kintsugi." This ancient technique was discovered in the 15th century and is the art of putting broken pottery pieces back together with gold. Broken objects are repaired with real gold powder to enhance and make them more beautiful instead of trying to hide the scars.

This philosophy resonated with me as a symbolic art of brokenness, resilience and healing. It is built on the ideology that by embracing our flaws and imperfections, we can recreate ourselves and become stronger and a more beautiful piece of art. Every broken part is unique, and instead of repairing any pieces of items fully, this technique highlights the *scars* as part of its unique design.

My self-esteem was so low at that point, and until I came across the Japanese word, I couldn't understand how there could ever be beauty in brokenness. Broken objects are usually discarded because they are of no use to humankind. I cried to God, telling Him I wasn't in a good place. God, can I really find beauty here? However, this metaphor illustrates every step of the healing process, whether physical or emotional.

Cared for and honoured, the broken object assumes its past and becomes more resilient, beautiful, and precious. The penny dropped; there was beauty in my brokenness. I had to endure the storms and the tough times to find healing and realise my full potential. Diamonds must go through the rigorous process of extreme pressure and heat before becoming shiny and beautiful.

Signs of brokenness

Here are a few signs of brokenness that you might relate to:

- A feeling of emptiness where you've run out of energy and zeal to keep going
- It seems like all hope is lost, faith is gone, and you are at the point of no return
- When you have no words, prayer or strength for action, brokenness may take over
- You are trying to figure out where God is
- Brokenness is when you feel beaten up, battered, broken and all alone

We don't always understand our brokenness. We don't want to or can't see the *beauty* in it, and that's okay. However, God uses broken objects, and in my life, I fully understand that finding beauty in brokenness comes by completely trusting Him. The perfect world expects us to hide our weaknesses, flaws and mistakes. Admitting we need help is one of the hardest tasks to do. This often renders us to invisible pride, powerlessness, shamefulness, being forgotten and rejected.

I often look back and ask God why He chose me to go through some of the painful periods in my life. Why did my parents have to die so young? Why did I have to lose my brother Michael? Why did my loved ones have to be plagued with illness? As much as these hurt me, I could almost hear that still small voice reminding me that I had to be broken to draw closer to becoming the masterpiece He destined me to be. Although my scars are profound, this brokenness is part of God's plan for my life.

Despite all the pain and setbacks in my life's journey, the meaning of *Beauty for Ashes* is clear. My Lord loves me more than anyone can ever do! Therefore, I am trying not to lose hope because God promises me that I will be compensated with beauty for all my troubles.

The following verse signifies His promise to me, and I hold on to this dearly:

"Provide for those who grieve in Zion to bestow on them a crown of beauty instead of ashes, the oil of joy instead of mourning, and a garment of praise instead of a spirit of despair. They will be called oaks of righteousness, a planting of the Lord to display His splendour."

Isaiah 61:3.

This verse perfectly explains the real essence of the phrase, *Beauty for Ashes*. It gives me a message of hope. No matter my trials, my suffering will be compensated with something beautiful beyond my wildest imagination. As humans, it's easy to be discouraged because of disappointments that we can't fully understand.

Life isn't always fair, but God says He will take what was meant for our harm and use it to our advantage. He will pay you back double for the unfair moments that happened. He will give you beauty for ashes, but you have to *let go of the ashes* before you receive the beauty. You're not going to understand everything that happens, but God does and always has a purpose. He knows how to bring good out of the bad, so let's keep pressing on!

Through my brokenness, I am trying hard to find the beauty in the hidden pieces. God created me in His image, and I am determined to use my brokenness to ignite hope in this dark world. There are daily questions and tears, and I still ask God why. The tears will always fall, though I trust, hope and wait in God's perfect timing. In the meantime, I am turning my mess into a message for other struggling mothers.

Fourteen years later, the babies who were pronounced at birth would live for under a year are very much here with us today! Jane, my very comical twin Angel, challenges and makes me cry and smile at the same time. - She loves to put on make-up and trying on new clothes. She loves parties, shopping, picking out each item on the aisle and carefully dropping them into the shopping trolley. When we arrive home, Jane insists on helping us unpack by putting the items in their rightful places. Jane has made incredible progress with her speech and understanding.

I always say that she is the most observant of my children. She instantly notices when mummy is down and will repeat the words "Mummy sad; mummy sad" to anyone who will listen. Occasionally when she caught me crying, she will go and find her daddy or sisters, hold their hands and bring them to me so they could see that I was in pain.

One moment, I had an awful day, and as I wept uncontrollably in the corner of my room, she walked in and, with the few words managed to master over the years said, "Mummy sad, mummy cry, mummy tissue."

She then walked away, went to the bathroom and got some tissue, but on her way back to the room, somewhere in her mind, she probably thought, mummy is crying too much for these tissues. So, she walked off in the direction of the airing cupboard and brought me a huge towel. As soon as I saw her coming towards me with the towel, I burst into laughter and carried on the day as I usually would. Jane filled my heart with joy, and the tears stopped.

As for Ivana, the seizures have hugely impacted her little body; regression has set in, and she has lost weight and the ability to utter most of the words she mastered. But she, too, continues to grow at her own pace and shows love in her way. For example, while Jane would go off and grab a towel, Ivana would gaze at me intently, lovingly take my hand and hold it in her little hand until I was calm.

This gesture melts my heart as I know my baby isn't saying anything at that point, but she sees my pain and loves me unconditionally. She teaches me that words are not needed to show she cares. Sometimes, all that is required is a touch, sitting close to a loved one when they have a bad day or simply holding a hand. I've learnt and found that there is so much beauty in these simple acts.

My Journey with Twin Angels

As far as special dietary requirements are concerned, that is a distant memory. From barely being unable to digest 1ml of breast milk, Ivana and Jane love their African food. At each meal, Jane will shout, "Pepper, pepper!" as she loves to have her meals served with black or green pepper, a Ghanaian delicacy.

This has been our journey thus far. The good, the bad and the ugly side of autism and epilepsy. It's been a painful process with many sleep-deprived nights, but I've come to accept that I am a work-in-progress and God's masterpiece. When we think of a masterpiece, we think of perfection. There are many occasions where I've not thought highly of myself, primarily as I've encountered situations that have broken me to the core.

No matter who you are or what you do, it's tough to see beauty in your brokenness, but that is where the beauty lies because although it may not seem or feel like it right now, God uses brokenness for His Glory. He uses brokenness to show us that we have no choice but to rely on His strength in our weakness.

Chapter NINE

-

Staying positive during trying times

The greatest glory in living lies not in falling, but in rising every time we fall.

Nelson Mandela.

Dealing with the challenges that come our way through the journey called life isn't easy, but we must grasp and have complete faith in every season. This too shall pass, the storms will pass, and you will find peace and joy. Thus, the real essence of life is learning from the challenges and not giving up. Additionally, some changes might be unsettling and will require discipline to stay positive during such times.

In 2021, after enduring much hurt and bottling up my feelings, I was on the verge of giving up, but I didn't. The phrase "Beauty for Ashes" gave me the hope to live and continue fighting for my children. Instead, I sought help and went to therapy. However, we all experience challenges that significantly impact our lives. As a result, we shouldn't compare our hardships to others because we're all on an individual journey and each battle is different.

I am not saying that handling the difficulties will be easy, but endeavour to remain hopeful because challenges make you a better person no matter how intense the circumstances are. The emphasis is on evolution which is beneficial since it strengthens you. So, always be positive and find what keeps you going.

It is a priority to surround yourself with people who have positive mindsets. If you don't know how to deal with your negative feelings, you will risk falling into depression that will endanger your wellbeing and make life difficult for your loved ones.

My Journey with Twin Angels

In my life, it seemed to me that I only had two choices; to live in sadness for the rest of my life or embrace my new normal as a special needs mum. For years, I chose to live in constant sorrow, but it cost me dearly. I became a shadow of myself, distant, and my personality changed during my walk-through with grief. My precious Angels are getting older, and as much as I would like to, I can't press the pause button to stop their growth. So, the years will carry on whether I want them to or not.

As time passes, I am learning that battles are won and lost in the mind. Instead of asking questions and wondering, "Why me?", I've decided to ask God for an easier, smoother, and realistic journey. I ask Him to grant us strength as we care for our angels. My daily actions, attitudes and habits are based mainly on what I allow my mind to feed on.

Negative thoughts suck away my strength and drain me physically, mentally and emotionally. Positive affirmations are the building blocks that give you and your child hope. The last few years have been tough, and as crazy as it sounds, I find joy in speaking positively about my circumstances. Whenever I have negative thoughts, I stop, take a few minutes, close my eyes, pray and repeat the affirmations to myself.

What are Affirmations?

Affirmations are positive statements repeated over time to influence or change a person's subconscious thinking. These can also be referred to as *positive power statements* or *I am's* since they are declarations that commonly begin with these words; for example, "I am a good friend."

In addition, many people find that affirmations are helpful when used as part of a mantra or meditation. The science of how affirmations work has much to do with psychology and the study of the human mind. Renowned neurologist; Sigmund Freud theorised that the human mind has three levels of awareness including the following:

1) **The *Conscious* Mind** – The conscious mind contains all of the thoughts, memories, feelings, and wishes of which we are aware at any given moment. This is the aspect of our mental processing that we can think and talk about rationally. This also includes our memory, which is not always part of our consciousness, but can be retrieved easily and brought into awareness. It includes what you are thinking about right now, whether it is in the front of your mind or the back. If you are aware of it then it's in the conscious mind

2) **The *Preconscious* Mind** – The preconscious mind contains information that can potentially be brought into the conscious mind. It can be retrieved with relative ease and usually be thought of as a memory or recollection

3) **The *Unconscious* Mind** – The unconscious mind contains thoughts, feelings, memories, and desires that are buried deep within ourselves below our conscious awareness. The unconscious mind contains contents that are unacceptable or unpleasant, such as feelings of pain, anxiety, or conflict. Even though we are not aware of their existence, they exert great influence on our behaviour

Freud likened the three levels of mind to an iceberg. The top of the iceberg that you can see above the water represents the conscious mind. The part of the iceberg that is submerged below the water, but is still visible, is the preconscious mind. The bulk of the iceberg that lies unseen beneath the waterline represents the unconscious mind.

Freud also estimated that the subconscious mind has approximately 50 - 60% of usage because it stores recent memories and information used daily such as habits and feelings. If you want to change your outlook on life or improve your mood, the subconscious mind is an important place to look.

Using Affirmations to improve your outlook
When a thought comes to mind on behalf of your child with special needs and they encounter barriers, it's easy to say "This is so

ridiculous and unfair!" However, these thoughts over time influence your brain to constantly look at the world in a way that's pessimistic, edgy and harsh to live in.

Creating a habit such as going to the gym takes regular commitment. It turns out that creating a positive thinking pattern is quite similar. Affirmations are typically the most helpful when they are repeated regularly and should be formed in the present tense. For example; "I am happy and confident" is preferable to "I will be happy and confident."

Similarly, it's important to believe in your affirmations. This is worth considering when you write affirmations in the present tense because you might not feel happy or confident at a certain point in time, which is okay, however, for your affirmations to be effective, you need to believe that you can be happy and confident, even if it takes a while to get there.

There are many ways to practice using affirmations in your life and may find it beneficial to take advantage of the different methods at once. While this won't necessarily speed the process of re-shaping your subconscious thoughts, it may help to keep you accountable for creating a habit of positive thinking. Let's look at the following examples:

- **I am my child's biggest hero** – You are your child's principal advocate; the one who fights every day to make his or her life a better one and gives strength to wake up every morning. You are the one who knows your child best

- **I will not apologise for my child's special needs** – I love my child because they are created in God's image. Therefore, I will ignore those who spread negativity about my child and correct them without creating unnecessary stress for myself. I will continue to be proud of my child

- **My child has something extraordinary to contribute to the world** – My child is unique and beautiful in their own way and brings joy to the world. With every smile, my child lights up the world. I know my child's positive impact on the world, and I will continue encouraging my child to shine

- **During difficult times, I will remain positive** – There are good days and bad days for my child. I will celebrate the good days and refuse to allow challenging moments to influence my thinking. I will remain optimistic, amid all the negativities because I believe that a tiny candle can brighten up a room

- **I will focus on what my child can do** – I will appreciate and celebrate every step and activity my child can do and help them learn in new ways. I will do my best to create opportunities for my child to develop in every way possible with the resources I have

- **I will never give up on my child** - My child can always count on me for support

- **Speak life to yourself** – If no one else tells you one positive affirmation, it's okay. Remember that you are always doing an amazing job as a special need's mum

- **I am not alone in this journey** – There are other people fighting along with me

- **I am an amazing mother** – My child is blessed to have me and I am blessed to have given birth to my child

- **My child is worth the hard work I put in** – Our progress from a week ago is worth celebrating

- **Avoid comparison** – I will not compare my non-verbal child to a developing child because they are two different people

- **Don't give up** – Just because my child isn't speaking yet doesn't mean they aren't intelligent; they are just communicating differently

Affirmations For Special Needs Mothers to avoid burnout
It's important for special needs mothers to carry out the following tasks from time to time:

- Doing the little tasks each day lifts my spirit and I'll complete them with diligence

- I will seek rest to take care of myself and my child

- I'm still a good mother even when I don't get everything on the list done

- I don't owe anyone an explanation for taking care of my specific needs

- I deserve to have my individual needs met without questioning. Therefore, I will not feel guilty for arranging a child minder or carer to pick up my child from therapy

- I'm a super mama! I am doing a great work in the early hours of the morning for my child

- Ensuring that my needs are met is just as important as ensuring that my child's needs are met

To be honest, I still cry about the future of Ivana and Jane and wonder whether they will be able to put full sentences together and communicate with us. Nonetheless, I hope they will catch up and the seizures stop. I pray that they can be independent and will go on to live their authentic and normal lives. HOPE is a word I thrive on and one which gets me through day by day.

Chapter TEN

-

Epilogue

I have a child with special needs. I didn't know if I would be strong enough. It turns out I am. And so are you.

Lisa Thornbury.

As I went on a walk one day, I noticed the leaves and trees had changed to a yellow-orange colour, and autumn was fast approaching. Autumn was a time of reflection, change and preparation for me. I sat on a bench by All-Saints Church, a spot often referred to by the locals as "Heaven on earth", looking over the picturesque village and began to reflect on the analogy my mother gave me about God's mysterious ways of using the four seasons – winter, spring, summer and autumn.

I'd gone to visit my mother in Ghana, and one night, way before my angels were born, I sat with her and wept as I recounted some challenges I was facing. Although she had nearly lost her ability to speak due to a neurological condition, she told me to reflect on my natural environment and observe a complex, yet wonderful world going through patterns and transitional phases.

My mother reminded me that nothing stays in its current state forever and there is a season for everything. In autumn, the leaves change colours. This happens yearly; however, it's so gradual that we don't realise it until we see the trees are orange, yellow, red and brown instead of green.

When winter approaches, the leaves fall from the trees. A few months later, spring brings forth new life and the cycle starts again. This happens all the time; the subtle, gradual, unseen changing and restorative seasons of life. My mother ended our conversation by saying; "This too shall pass;" a timely reminder that the difficult season I was going through wouldn't last. These words were the last I heard from my mother. The next time I saw her was in the morgue. Her last words and beautiful memories will forever be etched in my heart.

My story may differ from yours, but we all share unique and immense pain and sorrow to some degree. However, it's essential to remember that just as seasons change, so do the seasons of our lives change subtly. We go through trials which hurt us, and we heal, as it's part of the transitional process called *life*.

As I began to search myself for the challenges we've been through as a family and are still going through, I am reminded that each season is a signal that change is happening. Each season has brought me their own set of challenges, blessings and opportunities. Each season has stretched me and revealed more of my character as I've allowed it to shape me. Therefore, I am determined to walk into each season with an attitude of learning and growing.

Of course, I know first-hand how difficult it is to see the light when dealing with our children's unknown diagnoses and futures. The belief that something is permanent is terrifying and overwhelming but losing our sense of purpose will only leave us hopeless and damage our emotional well-being. So, on the days when I'm feeling extremely vulnerable and afraid, I pray and look at past experiences and challenges during my darkest moments and the tools used to deal with them.

This brings me to the realisation that although I am battered and bruised, God always makes a way. I won't pretend it's easy but working on my mindset and setting achievable targets has made my life more bearable. I say to myself that I will persist because I have a strong will to prosper, despite all the odds stacked against me.

Understanding what resilience means and finding coping mechanisms to encompass within our lives is a healing remedy for special needs mothers. I still go through sorrowful times when I cry. However, I've accepted that I am the mother to my Dynamic Twin Angels, Ivana and Jane. As difficult as this journey is, our Dynamic

My Journey with Twin Angels

Duo inspire us! They are full of life, and their regular antics and comical sibling rivalry bring great joy and laughter to us. They are energetic, have strong personalities, and have overcome many challenges. Ivana and Jane continue to defy all medical logic, labels and tags.

Little did I know, when God brought them to me, just how much they would change our lives. Our girls are on their missions. Our beautifully challenged angels have defied all medical odds since day one. They have fought for every breath they have and continue doing so. They continue to battle with sheer resilience of purpose and show no signs of giving up. They have taught me more in fourteen years than I've ever learned, and they still have lessons to teach the rest of the world.

They've taught me resilience and the ability to push harder. They've taught and shown me amazing unconditional love. They've taught me to persevere in the face of hardships and embrace an overwhelming amount of patience. They've taught me how to appreciate the little blessings, like a day without seizures and their giggles, dance moves and mischievous antics.

There are challenges to being a mother of special needs children, and society makes it even more challenging. I can't pretend that all is well with us, and at times, it can be tempting to be ungrateful that our precious angels have autism and epilepsy; for we have no idea what the future holds for them.

Nonetheless, I can say that we refuse to see a disability when we look at them. Instead, we see the adorable, precious and most beautiful blessings that we as a family could ask for. We've not forgotten the importance of HOPE. We are trying to keep hope and faith alive amid the turbulent storms.

> **Ivana and Jane's gifts may never earn money, but they remain my Crown of Jewels and Royal Diadems in God's Hands.**

My Journey with Twin Angels

Each day, I promise that I will celebrate the gifts they bring me and understand their ways of teaching, patience, compassion and unconditional love. Even at the expense of denial, hope is all I've got. I've realised how grateful I am for the strength gained from all the lessons learned. I am learning to step out of my comfort zone and speak my truth. In finding my voice and true inner worth, I will take the time to notice the beauty, innocence and light they bring into the world. I will worry less and celebrate them more for their unique gifts, and I am still hopeful that the storms will pass.

We all have a role to play in the world, and you can make a difference. Our children are here to teach us what we need to make life worthwhile. Find people who will support you on your challenging yet incredible journey. If you can't find your child's support, consider creating, developing, or starting it yourself.

Be part of the change you wish to see in the world. I am sharing my children's smiles and achievements, not to convince myself and others of their perfections, but simply as a mother whose children are her most prized possessions. The immense pain and frustration you are experiencing is a normal part of parenting children with additional needs.

We are still on our parenting journey, and although everything seems complex and hopeless, we are pressing on and moving forwards with our lives to the best of our ability. Finding the answers to all our questions isn't easy; however, as you search deeply enough, you will find easier ways to cope by using your inner resources and the relevant support systems you have managed to build around you.

"Find your true identity; dig deep within yourself and know that God created you for a greater purpose. Rise above your fears, limitations and boundaries; be hopeful, flourish, and live a purpose-filled life."

Against All Odds.

HELPFUL RESOURCES FOR PARENTS AND FAMILY MEMBERS

Attention Deficit Disorder
ADDISS – Information and support: www.addiss.co.uk

Angelman Syndrome
Angelman Syndrome Support Education and Research Trust – information, helpline, and newsletter: http://angelmanuk.org/

Autism and Asperger Syndrome
Ambitious about Autism – services, awareness-raising and campaigns: www.ambitiousaboutautism.org.uk/page/index.cfm

Anna Kennedy Online
Anna Kennedy offers information, training, advice and supports families with autism: www.annakennedyonline.com

Curly Hair Project
Information, support, training and resources:
www.thegirlwiththecurlyhair.co.uk

National Autistic Society
Information, support and schools: www.nas.org.uk

Research Autism
The only UK charity dedicated to research into interventions with autism: http://researchautism.net/pages/welcome/home.ikml

Talk about Autism
A safe and friendly online community:
www.talkaboutautism.org.uk

Caldwell Autism Foundation
Providing communication support to people on the autistic spectrum: http://thecaldwellfoundation.org.uk/

Royal College of General Practitioner
Childminders, parents and childcare staff may wish to hand this useful information about making the most of a visit to the GP to the parents of children with autism: www.rcgp.org.uk/clinical-and-research/clinical-resources/~/media/Files/CIRC/Autism/RCGP-Making-the-most-of-a-visit-to-your-GP-March-15.ashx

Autism West Midlands
The leading charity in the West Midlands for people with autism: www.autismwestmidlands.org.uk/

Autism Connect
An online social network for people with autism and their families: https://autism-connect.org.uk/site/index

The Autism Directory
Find autism-friendly resources in your local area and beyond. From CAMHS and coffee shops to SaLT's and special schools, you can find them on: www.theautismdirectory.com/default.asp?contentID=1

Child Autism UK
Support, advice and services for children with autism. See more information on their website: www.childautism.org.uk

Brain Injuries and Conditions

Advance: The Institute for The Scotson Technique
Unique restorative science for children and young people with brain injuries: www.scotsontechnique.com/

BIBIC (British Institute for Brain Injured Children)
Offers families practical help. Visit: www.bibic.org.uk/

Brainwave
Home-based programme for children with brain injuries/genetic conditions: www.brainwave.org.uk/

Cerebra
Support and information for families of children with brain-related conditions: www.cerebra.org.uk/

Child Brain Injury Trust
Provides information and support for the effects of 'traumatic' injury on a child's developing brain: www.childbraininjurytrust.org.uk/

Child Growth Foundation
Information about conditions causing growth problems: www.childgrowthfoundation.org/

Climb
Information for families of children living with inherited metabolic conditions: www.climb.org.uk/

Snowdrop
Provides neural developmental therapy for conditions including Cerebral Palsy, Autism, genetic conditions, developmental delay and brain injury: www.snowdrop.cc/

Cerebral palsy and Hemiplegia

Cerebral Palsy Guidance
Covers a wide range of topics, such as symptoms, causes, treatment and transitioning to adulthood: www.cerebralpalsyguidance.com

HemiHelp
Support for children and young people with hemiplegia (hemiparesis): www.hemihelp.org.uk/

Scope
Helpline and factsheets for parents: www.scope.org.uk

Chromosome Disorders

SOFT
Support for families affected by Patau's syndrome, Edwards syndrome, Partial Trisomy, Mosaicism and related disorders: www.soft.org.uk/

Unique
Information, networking and support for anyone affected by a rare chromosome disorder, their families and the professionals who work with them: www.rarechromo.org/html/home.asp

Genetic Alliance
Alliance of charities supporting children and families affected by genetic disorders: www.geneticalliance.org.uk

Cockayne Syndrome

Amy and Friends
Support and information for parents: www.amyandfriends.org

Cystic fibrosis

Cystic Fibrosis Trust
Information, advice, support and funding: www.cysticfibrosis.org.uk

Down's Syndrome

Down Heart Group
Information about associated heart conditions: www.dhg.org.uk/

Down's Syndrome Association
Information by life stages, support and helpline: www.downs-syndrome.org.uk/

Future of Down's
Online parenting support group: www.futureofdowns.com/

Downs Side Up
Links to resources and products that are useful for parents of children with Down Syndrome, as well as for practitioners: www.downssideup.com/p/essential-websites.html

Dyslexia and dyspraxia

Dyslexia-SpLD Trust (The)
A collaboration of voluntary and community organisations funded by the Department for Education to help children with dyslexia/SpLD to succeed in school: www.thedyslexia-spldtrust.org.uk/

Dyspraxia Foundation
Books, suggestions, teen newsletters, and adult support groups: www.dyspraxiafoundation.org.uk/

Epilepsy

Daisy Garland Trust
Focuses on children up to 12 with difficult-to-control epilepsy: www.thedaisygarland.org.uk/

Epilepsy Action
Information and support for children, adults and families: http://www.epilepsy.org.uk/

Young Epilepsy
Information and resources for young people: http://youngepilepsy.org.uk/

Klinefelter's Syndrome Association UK
Information and support: www.ksa-uk.net/

Rett UK
Information and support: www.rettuk.org

Sickle Cell Society
Information and counselling: www.sicklecellsociety.org/

Fragile X
Fragile X Society – support, information and helplines for families plus promotion of research: http://fragilex.org.uk/

Hearing Impairments

Elizabeth Foundation
Helping deaf preschool children learn to listen and talk: www.elizabeth-foundation.org/

National Deaf Children's Society
Help and support: www.ndcs.org.uk/

Heartline
Support and help for children with congenital heart conditions and their families.

Learning Difficulties and Disabilities

Mencap
Support and information for families and carers of children with a learning disability: www.mencap.org.uk/

SCOPE Online Community
Full of tips and bright ideas from parents, carers, teachers and therapists.

Easyhealth
Accessible health information for parents, supporters and carers of people with learning disabilities and people with milder learning disabilities themselves: www.easyhealth.org.uk/

Limb Conditions

REACH
Support and advice for children with hand or arm deficiencies and their parents: www.reach.org.uk/

Steps
Support for parents of children affected by lower limb conditions: www.steps-charity.org.uk/

Siblings Support

Sibs
www.sibs.org.uk

Young Sibs
https://www.youngsibs.org.uk/

Speech and Language Impairments

Afasic
Supports children with speech, language and communication impairments: www.afasic.org.uk/

I CAN
Supports speech, language and communication development in children: www.ican.org.uk/

Spina Bifida and Hydrocephalus

Shine
Information and advice including a helpline: www.shinecharity.org.uk/

Tourette's syndrome

Tourettes Action
Information and support: www.tourettes-action.org.uk

Turner syndrome

Turner Syndrome Support Society
Information and support: http://tss.org.uk

Undiagnosed Conditions

SWAN UK
Offers support and information to families of children with undiagnosed genetic conditions: http://undiagnosed.org.uk/

Visual Impairments

Calibre Audio Library
Provides audio books to those with sight impairment and dyslexia: www.calibre.org.uk/

Living Paintings
A free library of Touch to See books bringing to life the visual world for blind or partially sighted people: www.livingpaintings.org/

Load2Learn
Accessible textbooks and images to support dyslexic, partially sighted or blind learners: http://load2learn.org.uk/

LOOK UK
Supporting parents and carers of children with a visual impairment: www.look-uk.org/

MISE (Mobility and Independence Specialists in Education)
Holds a register of specialist practitioners who will deliver habilitation training to visually impaired children and young people: www.mise.org.uk/

National Blind Children's Society
Help and information for children and young people with visual impairments, and their families: www.nbcs.org.uk

Talking Books for Children
A free library of audiobooks for children from the RNIB: www.rnib.org.uk/talking-books-service

VICTA Visually Impaired Children Taking Action
Support for blind and partially sighted children, young people and their families: www.victa.org.uk/

Other Supportive Organisations

Additional Needs Alliance
Helping churches to include, support, create places of belonging and spiritually grow children, young people and adults with additional needs or disabilities: https://additionalneedsalliance.org.uk/

Anti-Bullying Alliance (ABA)
Information about bullying for parents and carers including Interactive Anti-Bullying Parent Information Tool: www.anti-bullyingalliance.org.uk/tools-information/advice-parents

Contact a Family
Links about different conditions: www.cafamily.org.uk/medical-information/conditions/
- **IPSEA** – training, support, webinars etc: www.ipsea.org.uk
- **Contact** – national freephone helpline for educational issues for parents who have children with SEND: www.contact.org.uk

My Journey with Twin Angels

Family Footings
A national project for families of disabled children with special educational needs. They provide advice and resources on how to use person-centred thinking to improve outcomes for children and young people in education, health care and day-to-day support. Parents can contact Family Footings to request free training in their school, children's centre or any other community setting: www.preparingforadulthood.org.uk/downloads/friends-relationships-and-community/family-footings.htm

Family Fund
Champions are an inclusive society where families with severely disabled or seriously ill children have choices and the opportunity to enjoy ordinary life: www.familyfund.org.uk/

FamilyLine
A free national helpline and befriender service: www.family-action.org.uk/familyline

Home-Start
Families struggling with post-natal depression, isolation, physical health problems, bereavement, special needs and many other challenges receive the support of a volunteer who will spend around two hours a week in a family's home supporting them in ways they need: www.home-start.org.uk/special-needs

Coping with a child who has a long-term illness or a physical disability can be a life-changing experience. Parents who are dealing with their own or their partner's medical condition can find life a real challenge. The Home-Start team may be able to support you. If you have received a diagnosis, are attending hospital appointments, or looking for financial help for medical equipment to adapt in your home, visit the website on: www.home-start.org.uk/disability-and-illness

Childrencape
Information and advice for parents and carers supporting children who have experienced bullying:
www.childrencape.org.uk/advice/advice-for-parents-and-carers/

NHS England
Range of resources, e.g., Ask Listen Do – Making conversations count in health, social care and education: Top tips for families

NHS Choices
Live Well: advice, tips and tools to help you make the best choices about your health and wellbeing https://www.nhs.uk/live-well/

SEND Gateway
Wide range of links, downloads, and events: www.sendgateway.org.uk, e.g., leaflet for parents with questions they can ask schools about how they support children with SEND www.sendgateway.org.uk/resources.nhs-England-ask-listen-do_1.html

SEND
Guide for parents and carers on the support system for children and young people with special educational needs and disability (SEND). Visit the website on: www.gov.uk/government/publications/send-guide-for-parents-and-carers

Special Needs Jungle
Range of information and links: www.specialneedsjungle.com

TUCK
Resource specifically for helping children and adults with autism to get better sleep: https://nevadaautism.com/autism-spectrum-disorder-asd-and-sleep/

Charities which give grants to families caring for a disabled child
Please note: There are grant-making organisations for specific disabilities, areas of the UK, occupations or faith applicants that haven't been included. You can search for these on our online grants information service or call the freephone helpline for information.

Disability Grants

Not every grant will be applicable to you and have only listed items that can be applied for below – most charities have a strict criteria about what they will fund - check before you apply. An application doesn't mean you are guaranteed a grant. We advise contacting more than one organisation for the items you need. Below, you will find useful information and links for your consideration:

1) Family Fund – Helping Disabled Children

- How to apply for essential items relating to the needs and wellbeing of a disabled, seriously ill child or young person and their family. This could include kitchen appliances, family breaks, laptops, furniture, bedding, clothing, hospital visiting costs, play equipment and many other items. In addition, there are grants for young people between the ages of 18 to 24. No grants for items which are the responsibility of the NHS or social services.

  Families in the UK raising a disabled or seriously ill child or young person up to the age of 17 with evidence of entitlement to statutory financial support have a separate application process for families residing in Wales. Parents and/or carers can apply. Application packs to be filled in and posted back to the Trust can be posted on request or downloaded from the website. If applying for the first time, you can register online via their website: https://www.familyfund.org.uk/grants-what-can-we-apply-for

Family Fund Telephone Number: **01904 550 055**

Type of grant_____

Eligibility criteria_____

How to apply for Mobility Equipment

2) Bruce Wake Charitable Trust

- This includes but not limited to adapted car seats, adapted buggies, adapted trikes, specialist seating systems, manual, powered and sports wheelchairs, wheelchair powerpacks, walking aids, portable hoists, tough furniture, Posturepedic sleep equipment, weighted blankets and sensory equipment. There are no grants for iPads, laptops, holidays, apps or communication aids. Disabled children and young people up to 25 must be in receipt of DLA.

  Applications must be for specialised pieces of equipment for individual children, not groups or schools, and must be made by the individual applying such as their parent or legal guardian. You will need to obtain a medical reference from a professional along with a quotation for the equipment. Contact the Trust to request an application form on the website which is: https://brucewaketrust.co.uk/grants/

Bruce Wake Charitable Trust Telephone Number: **03448 793 349**

Type of grant_____

Eligibility criteria_____

3) Newlife Charity for Disabled Children

- How to apply for grants towards disabled children. There are now around one million disabled and terminally ill children in the UK. Thousands of them rely on Newlife to get the equipment they need, equipment that has often been refused by the statutory services or the delays in provision mean that the child will suffer unnecessarily. Newlife runs the only fast track equipment services in the UK helping those children in urgent need.

Applications are processed only through a charitable organisation or equivalent, submitted with appropriate financial information and processed in a preliminary form on the website: https://newlifecharity.co.uk

Newlife Charity for Disabled Children Telephone Number: **01543 462 777**

Type of grant_____

Eligibility criteria_____

Alternatively, you can contact the Newlife Free Nurse Helpline Telephone Number on: **0800 902 0095**

4) The League of the Helping Hand

- How to apply for grants to provide financial assistance to those who are in hardship due to illness or disability. This includes physical and diagnosed mental health conditions, learning disabilities and people caring for an adult or child with a disability. You can apply online or call the Helpline number below if you need assistance. The Trust may request additional information.

The League of the Helping Hand Telephone Number: **01444236099**

Type of grant_____

Eligibility criteria_____

5) Carers Trust Fund

- How to apply for one-off grants of up to £250.00 towards items including essential household goods (excepting computers and I.T. equipment), extended financial assistance, specialist equipment and carer's break depending on funding. Applicants of any age experiencing financial hardship on a very low income are considered, providing they have an illness, physical disability, diagnosed mental health problem, learning disability or they care for an adult or child who is disabled. Applications by an employee of a professional agency includes social services, health services, housing association, Carers Centre or Citizen's Advice Bureau on behalf of the recipient.

The sponsor must ensure that all statutory entitlements, including Local Welfare Grants where eligible have been applied for before submitting an application. The sponsor also takes responsibility for the distribution of funds in the manner agreed by LHH.

6) Mobility Trust – Powered Wheelchairs and Scooters

- How to apply for powered wheelchairs and scooters for people unable to get them through statutory or charitable means. The Trust also provides the first three years' insurance and the first two years' servicing free of charge. Disabled people of any age who are residents in the UK are allowed to apply.

Mobility Trust Telephone Number: **0118 984 2588**

Type of grant_____

Eligibility criteria_____

7) Specialised Equipment grants

- How to apply for the full spectrum of specialised 1equipment such as electric wheelchairs, mobility aids and items including specialised computers and sensory toys, emergency and welfare appeals. You can also visit the website on http://www.lifeline4kids.org. Disabled children and young people from 0 to 18 can apply. Send an email indicating the specific requirement and costs, brief information about the child including their full name, date of birth, health conditions, family name, postal, email address and contact number to the email of: appeals@lifeline4kids.org. A form will be emailed or posted to the applicant.

8) Critical Household Funds

- How to apply for critical household items such as gas/electric cookers, furniture and kitchen equipment, clothing in exceptional or emergency situations, baby equipment, fridges and freezers, washing machines, children's beds and bedding. Maximum grant £300.00 and only one item per application is normally considered.

  Children aged 18 or under living with parents or carers can also apply and families/young people living in crisis. You can request a form by email either with the electronic or paper versions available. Applications must be made by a support worker that is supporting the family capable of assessing their needs, and who can administer a grant on behalf of Buttle UK.

9) EDF Energy Trust Domestic Gas and Electricity Grants

- How to apply for helping individuals and family's clear domestic gas and electricity debts, purchase essential energy efficient household items such as washing machines and cookers or with Bankruptcy / Debt Relief Order (DRO), Sequestration and Minimal Asset Process Fees.

  This also applies to individuals and families in need, poverty, those who are struggling to pay gas and electricity debts, and those who are currently domestic account holders of EDF Energy. The Trust strongly recommends seeking money/debt advice before applying to increase your chance of a successful application. See their website for more details on www.edfenergy.com.

EDF Energy Trust Telephone Number: **01733 421 060**

Type of grant_____

Eligibility criteria_____

10) Buttle UK Grants
- Buttle UK is named after Reverend Frank Buttle, a remarkable man whose hard work and personal sacrifice helped to establish our grant programmes, which have been helping children and young people in need across the UK since 1953.

Buttle UK Telephone Number: **020 7828 7311**

Type of grant_____

Eligibility criteria_____

11) Cares Trust Grants of up to £300.00
- How to apply for grants of up to £300.00 for essentials including breaks for carers (with or without the person they care for), items for the home including white goods, driving lessons and other travel costs relating to caring roles, courses and materials to develop carers' skills, home repairs and short-term or time-limited replacement care. This applies to carers aged 16+ and can be contacted by the local carer services for advice. Applicants will need to complete a supporting statement. Find your nearest Carers Centre or scheme on the website: http://carers.org.

Carers Trust Telephone Number: **0300 772 9600**

Type of grant_____

Eligibility criteria_____

12) React Specialist Medical Support

- How to apply for specialist medical, mobility and educational equipment, specialist furniture and homeware including white goods, travel and subsistence expenses, respite breaks and holidays, and end-of-life support including funeral expenses and those who are financially disadvantaged and have families caring for a child with a life-limiting illness. Applicants can download the form from the React website on www.reactcharity.org or request one by email or telephone. Parents and guardians may apply, but the form must be endorsed by a medical or healthcare professional:

React Telephone Number: **020 8940 2575**

Type of grant_____

Eligibility criteria_____

13) Equipment for Independent Living

- How to apply for Equipment for Independent Living. This helps people who have disabilities aged 16+ and living in the UK. Grants are used for equipments including wheelchairs, adjustable beds and communication aids. Applications are considered at quarterly meetings and a health professional would need to support the application and confirm that the applicant needs the equipment requested. More information can be found by visiting Equipment for Independent Living via their address:

Address: Honorary Secretary
Equipment for Independent Living
19 Flanchford Road
London
W12 9ND

14) Independence at Home

- Providing grants to people of all ages who have a physical or learning disability or long-term illness and who are in financial need. Independence at Home is a charity that provides grants to people of all ages who have a physical or learning disability or long-term illness and who are in financial need. This financial help enables them to obtain mobility and disability equipment, home adaptations and other essential items to make an immediate, practical and positive effect on daily life at home.

Independent at Home Telephone Number: **0208 427 7929**

Type of grant_____

Eligibility criteria_____

15) The Ogilvie Charity

- How to apply for financial help towards the cost of essential items to improve independence, comfort, safety and quality of life at home. One-off grants for specialist disability, mobility, communication equipment, furniture, home adaptation, repair, kitchenware including white goods, homeware, therapeutic toys, play equipment, heating costs (winter months only) and sundry other expenses. Grants can only be made towards items not covered by statutory provisions.

  Applicants with physical, neurological or sensory impairments in the UK who are living at home and in financial need can also apply. Visit the website on https://www.ogilviecharities.org.uk to see the list of eligible conditions before applying. Applications must be submitted on behalf of the applicant by a social care professional who is in contact with you or a family member:

Address: The Ogilvie Charities
The General Manager
The Gate House
9 Burkitt Road
Woodbridge
Suffolk
IP12 4JJ
Telephone Number: **01394 388 746**

Type of grant_____

Eligibility criteria_____

16) Glasspool Charity Trust

- How to apply for one-off grants in the region of £100.00 to £200.00 for individuals to purchase essential items not supplied by the statutory agencies. For example, beds and bedding, cookers, fridges, freezers, washing machines, powered disability aids for wheelchair users and in very limited circumstances, clothing.

  This also includes grants in the region of £100.00 to £300.00 for respite holidays for carers and family holidays in the UK if funds allow. This applies to anyone of any age in poverty and carers. Applicants can send an email or post their forms through a social worker, community nurse or professional agency and would need to include full details of weekly household income and expenditure, other agencies being approached, and details of the items. Contact number below:

Glasspool Charity Trust Telephone Number: **020 3141 3161**

Type of grant_____

Eligibility criteria_____

17) Variety Children's Charity – White Goods and Household Items

- How to apply for white goods, beds and bedding, essential household items and other household goods, clothing and school uniforms. Flooring where there is an exceptional circumstance for disabled people, educational computer equipment, and television where there's permanent or a substantial disability.

The Trust expects all applicants to have applied to their Local Welfare Schemes and charities before filling out the form. The Trust will not make a grant where there's a reasonable expectation that funding is available from other sources, particularly statutory funds. Applicants can visit the Trust's website on htttps://www.variety.org.uk for more details.

Variety Children's Charity Telephone Number: **020 7428 8100**

Type of grant_____

Eligibility criteria_____

18) Whizz Kidz Grants for Medical Equipment

- How to apply for grants of £100.00 to £6,000.00 for medical equipment such as monitoring equipment, feeding tubes, hoists, sensory play or mobility equipment for a nursery or playgroup, manual, powered and sports wheelchairs for children (via a separate form). This grant provides days out and trips for children and is applicable for sick, disabled, disadvantaged and young people up to the age of 18 who are permanently residing in the UK.

Applications can be made by parents and medical professionals on behalf of individual children and must be supported by an appropriate medical professional, e.g., an occupational therapist, physiotherapist or paediatrician, clarifying the equipment sought and how it would benefit the children. Children over 13 years can apply for a wheelchair grant themselves and forms are downloadable from the website on https://www.whizz-kidz.org.uk. Two quotations for the items requested should accompany the application.

Whizz Kidz Telephone Number: **0800 151 3350**

Type of grant_____

Eligibility criteria_____

19) Cauldwell Children Grants for Mobility Equipment

- How to apply for funds on behalf of mobility equipment up to the value of £2,500.00 for physically disabled children and young people, such as manual and powered wheelchairs, buggies, and sport wheelchairs under some circumstances. Children and young people under 18 years with a physical disability can apply.

  Funding is only available where the applicant's local NHS Wheelchair Service doesn't provide equipment to meet the child's essential mobility needs. Only the parent/legal guardian of the child/young person may apply. Applicants can apply online or download an application pack on https://www.caudwellchildren.com.

Cauldwell Children Telephone Number: **0345 300 1348**

Type of grant_____

Eligibility criteria_____

20) Percy Bilton Charity – Mobility and Sensory Equipment Grant

- How to apply for mobility, sensory equipment and therapies for autistic children. This grant provides 70% to 80% of the total cost of mobility and disability sports equipment. Families will need to put money towards it or find another charity who can help with the cost. Grants towards Selective Dorsal Rhizotomy (SDR) Surgery and Post-SDR Rehabilitative Physiotherapy and other treatments may not be available on the NHS website.

  Parents or carers' training must ensure that the effects of treatment and therapy programmes are maximised. Children under 19 years with a chronic illness or disability can apply. Parents and guardians must be living legally in the UK and be earning less than £45,000 before tax each year, excluding benefits. Applicants can apply online or download the application form on the website which is https://www.percy-bilton-charity.org. Applications need to be supported by an Occupational Therapist or Physiotherapist.

Percy Bilton Charity Telephone Number: **020 8579 2829**

Type of grant_____

Eligibility criteria_____

21) Dreams Come True Grants

- How to apply for Dreams Come True grants works with families to enrich the lives of children and young people with severe and life-limiting conditions. Children and young people between the ages of 2 to 21 who are seriously ill or have a life-limiting condition are eligible to apply.

  They must not have a request in progress with a similar organisation. If urgent, use the enquiry form on their contact page which is https://www.dreamscometrue.uk.com for a child with a prognosis and receiving palliative care. Children and young people can be nominated by their parents, extended family members, medical professionals, social workers and friends, or can nominate themselves.

Dreams Come True Charity Telephone Number: **01428 726 330**

Type of grant_____

Eligibility criteria_____

22) Happy Days Children's Charity Funds for organised day trips and events

- How to apply for funds and day trips, events, activity holidays for groups of children and young people, and families throughout the UK. Typical activities include the seaside, zoo, theme parks, safari parks, fun fairs and trips to the theatre. Children between the ages of 3 to 17 years with learning difficulties, physical or mental disabilities are eligible, as well as young people that've been abused, bereaved or act as carers for a parent or sibling.

  Parents, family members and health professionals can apply for family respite breaks. Organisations can apply for group days out and activity holidays. Visit the website on: https://www.happydayscharity.org/applications

Address: Happy Days Children's Charity
Unit 6 - 7 The Glover Centre
23 - 25 Bury Mead Road
Hitchin
Hertfordshire
SG5 1RP
Happy Days Children's Charity Telephone Number: **01462530710**

23) Make a Wish Grants for children and young people

- How to apply for grants for children and young people with critical illnesses. Any UK resident child or young person between the ages of 3 to 17 who is living with a critical illness are eligible. The child must not receive any other wish-granting organisation.

  The Foundation accepts referrals from parents or guardians, medical professionals, and will speak to each child's consultant to establish whether their condition is medically classed as critical. Applicants can apply on the website: https://www.make-a-wish.org.uk/wishes/wish-eligibility/

Make a Wish Foundation UK Telephone Number: **01276 405 070**

Type of grant_____

Eligibility criteria_____

24) Ray of Sunshine Grants for children with life-limiting illnesses

- How to apply for grants on behalf of children with serious or life-limiting illnesses. Grants wishes includes hospital ward wishes, organising outings and large-scale events can apply for children residing in the UK with life-limiting illnesses between the ages of 3 to 18 years. **Note**: Applications will be accepted until the day before the child's 19th birthday. Visit the website on https://raysofsunshine.org.uk.

Rays of Sunshine Children's Charity Telephone Number: **020 8782 1171**

Type of grant_____

Eligibility criteria_____

25) When You Wish Upon a Star Grants for children with life threatening illnesses
- How to apply for grants on behalf of children with life threatening and terminal illnesses between the years of 3 and 18 can apply and must not have a Wish granted by another Charity. Parents, guardians or health professional can nominate a child by filling out the online form on: https:www.whenyouwishuponastar.org.uk.

When You Wish Upon a Star Telephone Number: **0115 979 1720**

Type of grant_____

Eligibility criteria_____

26) General Grants Lists
- How to apply for one-off dreams grants to children who are terminally or seriously ill, including trips of a lifetime or the chance to meet a celebrity. This grant also includes items that make a difference to family such as medical equipment, home adaptations or a wheelchair. Children from 0 to 18 years who have a terminal condition can apply. Parents or legal guardians must download and complete an application form on the website which is: https://contact.org.uk/general-grants-list

27) Grants Search – Heinz, Anna and Carol Kroch Foundation
- This fund is only open to applications from intermediaries or support workers. Grants to help people on a very low income who may also have medical problems, who have recently experienced domestic violence or are homeless. If an applicant is experiencing financial problems, they must seek someone in a professional capacity (social worker, Citizens Advice Bureau, local authority or charity etc.) to act on their behalf and submit the application. The charity does not accept self-referrals.

Address:
The Heinz, Anna and Carol Kroch Foundation.
Beena Astle,
Administrator, Heinz, Anna & Carol Kroch Foundation,
PO Box 327
Hampton
London
TW12 9DD
Telephone Number: **020 8979 0609**

Type of grant_____

Eligibility criteria_____

References

Chapter Two
- https://www.healthline.com/health/lactic-acidosis
- https://www.nlm.nih.gov/medlineplus/ency/article/000391.htm
- https://en.wikipedia.org/wiki/Lactic_acidosis

Chapter Three
- https://www.midwiferytoday.com/mt-articles/kangaroo-care-work/

Chapter Four
- https://www.autism.org.uk/advice-and-guidance/what-is-autism
- https://www.thelilyfoundation.org.uk/get-informed/questions-answers/#faq-17
- https://www.cdc.gov/ncbddd/autism/mitochondrial-faq.html
- https://www.hamiltonhealthsciences.ca/wp-content/uploads/2019/08/MitochondrialDiseaseUnderstanding-lw.pdf
- https://www.henryford.com/blog/2016/05/children-epilepsy-10-tips-parents-caregivers
- https://www.healthline.com/health/celebrities-epilepsy
- https://www.appliedbehavioranalysisprograms.com/historys-30-most-inspiring-people-on-the-autism-spectrum/

Chapter Five
- https://assets.publishing.service.gov.uk/government/uploads/system/uploads/attachment_data/file/1082518/Special_educational_needs_publication_June_2022.pdf
- http://www.kargacademy.com/lee-s-thoughts/grieving-the-loss-of-the-perfect-child
- https://www.verywellmind.com/five-stages-of-grief-4175361

Chapter Six
- https://onlinelibrary.wiley.com/doi/pdf/10.1002/casp.2602 J Community Appl Soc Psychol. 2022;32:936–948.

Chapter Seven
- http://www.kargacademy.com/lee-s-tips/creating-success-at-home

Chapter Eight
- https://childmind.org/article/advice-siblings-of-special-needs-kids/

Chapter Nine
- https://www.simplypsychology.org/unconscious-mind.html
- https://opentextbc.ca/introductiontopsychology/chapter/2-2-psychodynamic-and-behavioural-psychology/
- https://www.verywellmind.com/the-conscious-and-unconscious-mind-2795946

Chapter Ten
- https://newsday.co.tt/2019/01/07/special-needs-parents-affirmations/
- https://unlimitedplay.org/10-encouraging-affirmations-for-parents/

www.ingramcontent.com/pod-product-compliance
Lightning Source LLC
Chambersburg PA
CBHW032112040426

42337CB00040B/229